Finance and Accounting
for Managers

David Davies is principal lecturer in financial management at the University of Portsmouth. A qualified accountant with a masters degree in management from Henley Management College, he previously spent 17 years in the private and public sectors with GEC, Thomas De la Rue, IBM and several local authorities. He currently lectures on DPM, MBA, DMS and undergraduate courses as well as undertaking consultancy work. He is the author of *The Art of Managing Finance* published by McGraw-Hill in 1992.

The Institute of Personnel and Development is the leading publisher of books and reports for personnel and training professionals and students and for all those concerned with the effective management and development of people at work. For full details of all our titles please telephone the Publishing Department on 0181 263 3387.

Management Studies Series

Series Editors: Michael Armstrong and David Farnham

The IPD examination system provides a unique route into professional personnel practice. The Management Studies Series provides the essential core texts at both levels.

Case Studies in Personnel
ed. Diana Winstanley and Jean Woodall

Tutors' Manual
ed. Diana Winstanley and Jean Woodall

Passing Your IPM Exams
Elaine Crosthwaite

Management Studies 1

Finance and Accounting for Managers
Second Edition
David Davies

The Corporate Environment
Second Edition
David Farnham

Management Information Systems and Statistics
Roland and Frances Bee

Management Processes and Functions
Michael Armstrong

Managing Human Resources
Second Edition
Jane Weightman

Management Studies 2

Employee Development
Rosemary Harrison

Employee Relations
David Farnham

Employee Resourcing
Derek Torrington, Laura Hall,
Isabel Haylor and Judith Myers

MANAGEMENT STUDIES 1

Finance and Accounting for Managers

David Davies

Second Edition

Institute of Personnel and Development

To Ann, for her help and support

First published in 1990
Reprinted 1990
Second edition 1994
Reprinted 1995

Phototypeset by The Comp-Room, Aylesbury
and printed in Great Britain by Short Run Press Ltd., Exeter.

British Library Cataloguing-in-Publication Data
A catalogue record for this book is available from the British Library

ISBN 0-85292-527-1

**INSTITUTE OF PERSONNEL
AND DEVELOPMENT**
IPD House, Camp Road, London SW19 4UX
Tel: 0181 971 9000   Fax: 0181 263 3333
Registered office as above. Registered Charity No. 1038333
A company limited by guarantee. Registered in England No. 2931892

Contents

List of figures

Editors' Foreword

Today's business environment demands that managers possess a wide range of knowledge, skills and competencies. As well as a sound understanding of management processes and functions, managers need to be able to make the best use of their time and talents, and of other people's, and to work with and through others to achieve corporate objectives. They also need to demonstrate a full understanding of the business environment and of their organization's key resources: its people, finance and information.

Management education in Britain has at last begun to take full account of these business realities. In particular, the Professional Management Foundation Programme is a major initiative developed by a group of forward-looking professional institutes to meet these needs. They recognize that a synthesis of knowledge and skills, and theory and practice, is vital for all managers and those aspiring to management positions.

The Institute of Personnel and Development is strongly committed to developing professional excellence. This major series reflects this ideal. It covers five key areas: management processes and functions; the corporate environment; managing human resources; management information systems and statistics; and finance and accounting for managers. In drawing on the expertise of experienced teachers and managers, this series provides all students of management with an invaluable set of practical, introductory and informed texts on contemporary management studies.

MICHAEL ARMSTRONG
DAVID FARNHAM

Chapter 1

Introduction

Organizations require many resources to enable them to operate successfully in an environment that is competitive and frequently openly hostile. In the private sector the success of an organization can be measured in different ways, including its ability to make profits, generate cash, capture market share or provide a service.

The public sector has often found difficulty in justifying the work that it undertakes on the grounds that there is 'no profit motive'. This has dramatically changed in recent years, with value-for-money audits, direct works organizations having to compete in the open market for contracts and compulsory competitive tendering applying to all parts of the organization.

The new climate confirms that the public and private sectors have to compete for scarce resources to enable them to operate at all, and if they are to grow they have to be seen to be performing successfully in order to attract those resources. Both the public and private sectors require people, materials, machinery, equipment, buildings, money and information. Although each of these is important, this book is mostly concerned with how the Personnel Manager employs financial resources. The decisions of such managers and others are translated into the international language of money, which gives a common understanding of plans and enables the performance of organizations, and individuals within those organizations, to be monitored and controlled. This cannot be achieved, however, without frequent and accurate financial information in the right form reaching the right people at the right time to enable them to make good use of it. Personnel managers, among many others, need to keep a close eye on the cash position. The way in which money moves through a manufacturing concern may be illustrated by the way in which water flows through a series of reservoirs and pipes (figure 1).

The reservoirs of inventory, capital, work in progress, finished goods and debtors represent traps in which money may build up. If they are allowed to become too large, cash-flow problems will result. The

1

Figure 1
Where the money goes in a manufacturing concern

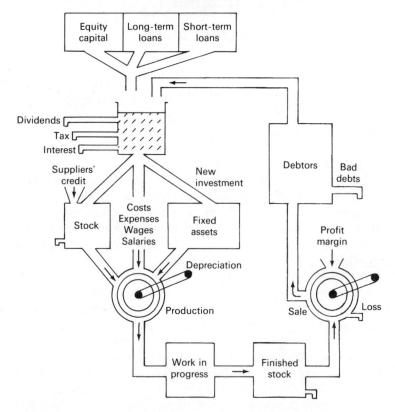

management information system should therefore highlight these possible problems, so that management is made aware of them early enough for remedial action to be taken to correct the situation before it becomes serious. Good management practice, which is represented by the pumps, supported by useful, timely information, ensures that any delays which occur are kept to an absolute minimum.

The public sector is under exactly the same pressures to ensure that the best possible use is made of the people, money and other resources available to it, and that no hold-ups occur in the efficient running of the organization. Both sectors are responsible for planning their activities and controlling actions as they take place, so that targets are met and the instructions of management carried out. Personnel managers ensure that organizational goals are achieved through its people. Failure to perform to the required standard leads to job losses and possibly to the demise of the organization. Sources of finance may show a different emphasis, with much of the public-sector money coming from the business rate, council tax and government grants, whilst the private sector is responsible for obtaining its resources direct from the public. They both provide goods and services with the monies obtained, and compete in the provision of such services as old people's and children's homes, refuse collection and housing maintenance, as well as housing itself.

Figure 2
Where the money goes in a non-manufacturing organization

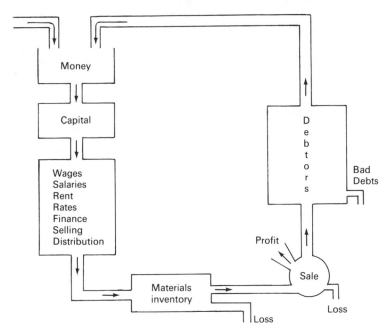

In view of this commonality, figure 2 is appropriate to both the non-manufacturing private sector and the non-manufacturing public sector of the economy. We can see that for all organizations the control of levels of stock/inventory and debtors is extremely important. The ways in which this control may be achieved are discussed later in the book, but the efficiency of the organization depends on the correct information being available in the right place, at the right time, and then being promptly acted upon by properly trained people.

This book has been written to give personnel practitioners a clear understanding of the processes outlined above, and of the role of financial and cost accounts and how they may be employed to clarify the financial performance of organizations and aid decision making.

The next three chapters explore the role of financial management. Chapters 5–8 discuss specific financial statements, whilst the remainder of the book looks at the role of costing in the process of planning and control in which the Personnel Manager becomes involved.

Chapter 2

The Finance Function

The primary role of the finance function of an organization is to ensure that financial resources are obtained at a minimum cost and that they are used effectively by all concerned. The Financial Manager is responsible for attempting to achieve this objective and in doing so breaks it down into three main decisions, each of which we will discuss in turn.

The financing decision

This is the first major decision of the organization. What sources are to be used to obtain finance and in what proportions? In the private sector the amount that can be raised by the issue of shares or by borrowing is limited by the Articles and Memorandum of Association. None the less the proportions in which the money is raised through the issue of shares or in other ways has an impact on the cost of the resources as well as on the public's perception of the firm. Companies that borrow a high proportion of their financial resources as opposed to issuing shares are said to be highly geared or leveraged and are perceived to be high-risk concerns.

The ways in which organizations in the public sector can obtain finance are laid down by statute and they are constrained by the principle of *ultra vires*. This means that certain actions are beyond their powers, and sets boundaries within which the organization must function. Nevertheless the head of the financial department has a good deal of discretion in deciding where borrowed monies should be obtained, although there is obviously clear public accountability.

The investment decision

The second major decision is how the funds that the organization has

5

obtained should be invested. Here again the private sector has rather more discretion than the public, which has a statutory duty to provide such services as public health and housing. The Financial Manager, in conjunction with the Personnel Manager and other members of the management team, has to decide how much should be invested in fixed assets like land and buildings, plant and machinery and equipment, and how much in current assets like inventory or stock.

The asset management decision

The Financial Manager helps to decide how the assets that have been acquired should be managed. It is in the nature of organizations that once fixed assets have been acquired they normally remain *in situ* for several years. This tends to make managers concentrate their attention in the short term on current asset management.

The management team works together in the management of the assets, with the Personnel Manager responsible for managing both the normal departmental assets and the most valuable assets that any organization possesses—its people. We are not able to put an inventory value on people, but companies such as Marks and Spencer which makes special efforts to manage and motivate their staff invariably see the results coming through on the bottom line.

The management information system

The Financial Manager has another important role to play, and that is operating the financial information system. The majority of organizations now have a computerized system that shows managers how well they are operating against plan. This information is usually produced monthly, although it can be done more frequently, and it is the Financial Manager's responsibility to ensure that the information is up to date, received on time and accurate. It is no good informing the Personnel Manager that the department is £20,000 over budget three months after the end of the year to which the information relates. By then it is too late to take any remedial action.

The Personnel, Financial and other managers should discuss the information they require in order to run their departments effectively. (Examples of how finance fits into the overall organizational structure in the private sector and a local authority are shown in figure 3.) Once this is known the timing and detail of the information should be agreed. It is no use the system producing a thirty-page report if only four pages are being used, not only because it is a waste of paper but more importantly because it is an ineffective use of a manager's time to be looking at information that is not relevant to the job in hand.

Figure 3
Finance on the Organization Chart

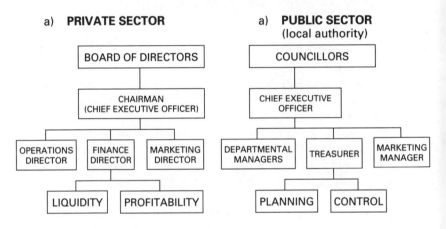

a) **PRIVATE SECTOR**   a) **PUBLIC SECTOR**
                                  (local authority)

So we can see that the Financial Manager is responsible for raising money as cheaply as possible and using it effectively within the context of the organization that is being served. In order to achieve this the objective of the organization must be known so that the context within which management is operating is clear.

Chapter 3

Sources and Uses of Money

Figure 1 in chapter 1 showed the three types of finance required by organizations, and they will now be considered in turn.

Permanent equity/capital

This is the money provided by the organization or its owners, which does not have to be repaid whilst the organization continues as a going concern.

In the private sector the money provided by the owners is in the form of share capital, and profits that have been retained in the organization, when it has traded successfully, become reserves. The share capital can be broken down into various types of shares. The ordinary share capital is the equity capital and gives the holder the right to vote on the way in which the organization should operate. The wishes of the shareholders are carried out by their elected representatives, the Board of Directors, and each Director would normally be expected to hold a large number of ordinary shares in that company. Directors who did not hold a large number of shares would be viewed with suspicion, as it would seem that they had no confidence in the organization they were running. The company is under no obligation to buy back any of the shares that it has sold, although it may decide to do so. The normal means of recovering money invested in an organization through the purchase of shares is by selling those shares to a purchaser through the medium of the stock exchange.

The ordinary shareholders, or equity holders, carry the biggest risk of all those who provide money for an organization. There is no stated rate of return on their investment, and if the company does not do well they get no return. They are the last to receive a return on their investment and the last to be paid in the event of failure, ranking after all the other creditors, secured or unsecured.

There are other shareholders who provide permanent capital. They are called preference shareholders and, as the name implies, they are in a preferential position *vis-à-vis* the ordinary shareholders, with regard to the receipt of dividends and the return of their money should the business fail. In view of this reduced risk the preference shareholders do not normally have voting rights when major decisions concerning the running of the company are made. Preference shares, like ordinary shares, can be bought and sold through the stock exchange.

The purpose of the stock exchange is to act as a market-place and bring together the providers and users of capital. Companies that wish to be listed on the exchange must have a proven record of profitability over a number of years and submit to a thorough investigation by the stock exchange before the privilege is granted. Those companies that are listed find their ability to raise permanent capital greatly enhanced, provided market conditions are conducive to the issue of shares.

Companies that wish to raise money through the issue of shares usually make use of the services of an issuing house, which will give advice on the timing and size of the issue and the price at which the shares should be issued. Press advertisements give details of the issue and invite applications for the purchase of shares. Payment is normally required in more than one instalment or tranche; for example, if the shares were to be sold for £1.50 each, payment might be requested as 50p on application, 50p on first call and 50p on second and final call, so that it could be three or four years after they had been received before the shares were fully paid for. Individuals wishing to sell shares they already own would also use the stock exchange, but they would employ the services of a stockbroker rather than an issuing house.

The permanent capital having been raised, it is the responsibility of the management of the organization to ensure that it is put to good use immediately. The purpose for which it was raised would have been stated at the time the public was invited to invest, and business should be started as quickly as possible if criticism is to be avoided which might make it difficult to raise money in the future.

Permanent capital may be needed to build or expand an organization through the purchase of fixed assets, such as plant and machinery, land and buildings, fixtures and fittings, or through the purchase of another company. On the other hand, it might be used to increase the working capital, which is what enables an undertaking to keep running until it earns some more money from its operations, and out of which all its running expenses are met.

Working capital is tied up in inventory, debtors and the bank, and lack of it severely restricts an organization's ability to operate successfully. The injection of fresh working capital can lead to increased operating levels, giving increased profitability and hence additional retained profits.

Long-term capital

The long-term capital consists of borrowed monies which will remain in the company for five or more years, and sometimes carries the option of being converted into ordinary share capital at the discretion of the lender. Normally, long-term loans are secured by a charge on the fixed assets of the borrowing concern, so that if things do not go well the lenders are certain of recovering their money through the sale of the fixed assets if necessary. Only the most successful organizations, like Marks & Spencer or GEC, are able to raise loans that are not secured on their fixed assets, as lenders feel that their money is safe with them and that the conditions on which it is lent will be honoured in full.

Loans may be raised through the stock market, particularly if they are to be convertible loans, but more usually the services of the other institutions of the City of London would be employed. If may be possible to raise money through one of the clearing banks, such as Barclays, Lloyds, Midland or National Westminster, but it should be remembered that they are not normally providers of venture capital and look for absolute security in their lending. Recent events have demonstrated, however, that they are not infallible.

More likely sources of long-term capital are the merchant banks, which specialize rather more in the provision of venture capital, but would still take an extremely close look at the organization's prospects and any available security before lending money.

The pension funds are always looking for good investment opportunities, but they too prefer safe investments, both from the point of view of income—that is the dividend received—and from that of capital growth—the increase in the value of the investment. They are prohibited from lending money. There are also quasi-governmental bodies, like 3i (Investors in Industry),* which have been set up specifically to provide capital as part of a policy to ensure that there is backing available to support good organizations and good ideas. The Business Expansion Scheme also exists to bring together organizations that

* 3i are at present becoming a public company (i.e. floating).

require capital and those prepared to provide it, facilitated by special tax provisions to attract the providers of capital. This now seems to be nearing the end of its useful life.

These are the main providers of long-term capital, but there are others; the list is by no means comprehensive. It should be remembered that, wherever the capital is obtained, the lender will need to be assured of its safety. The less security there is, the higher will be the charge for the money, if it can be obtained at all. A secured loan may be obtained at 7 per cent but an unsecured loan could cost as much as 13 per cent, and to make that worth while the user should ensure that at least 16 per cent is being earned—a requirement beyond most organizations.

Borrowed money can be used either externally or internally, i.e. to repay previous borrowings or, within the organization, to enable it to operate more effectively. Whatever is done must be perceived as being to the benefit of the borrowing organization, otherwise it will prove to be both difficult and expensive to raise further funds in the future.

Short-term capital

Short-term capital, in the form of loans that have to be repaid within five years, can be raised from the same sources and on broadly similar terms as long-term capital, although there will be differences in the rate of interest charged. The expertise of the financial management function is tested when borrowing money, in that it is its job to obtain the best possible terms, whilst the lenders will be endeavouring to achieve the same for themselves. When interest rates are high the lenders will want to lend for as long as possible and at a fixed rate of interest, whilst the borrower will want the loan to be for as short a term as possible and at a variable rate of interest, in the expectation that it will quickly fall.

The amount of borrowing and the terms on which money is lent will be decided largely by the City's view of the organization and its present capital structure, that is to say, the proportion of borrowed money in relation to that belonging to the owners. Where the proportion of borrowing is large, the organization is said to be 'highly geared' and it may be extremely difficult to borrow any further money.

The question of gearing is complex but we can say that the more highly geared an organization is, the greater the risk a prospective lender is taking and the higher the return that will be expected. A general rule

Finance and Accounting for Managers

with respect to the use of borrowed monies is that one should not borrow short to invest long. This means that short-term borrowing should not be invested in fixed assets, because if it were, it might be necessary to sell the fixed assets when the time came to repay the loan. Generally short-term borrowing should be employed in short-term investment, so that if necessary the money can be obtained easily when it has to be repaid.

These principles apply to both the private and the public sectors when they wish to raise money through the market-place, except that local authorities are generally seen as more secure places in which to invest money. None the less they still have to compete in terms of interest.

The proportion of funds that is obtained directly through the institutions of the City of London varies between the public and private sectors, in that in local government a large proportion of the money is obtained through the council tax, the business rate and government grants. Figure 4 shows how Hampshire County Council was funded in a recent financial year.

Figure 4
Hampshire County Council Funding

	%	
Specific Grant	18	
Rate Support Grant	32	
National Non Domestic Rate	31	(Business Rate)
County Precept	19	(Charge on Local Authorities within Hampshire

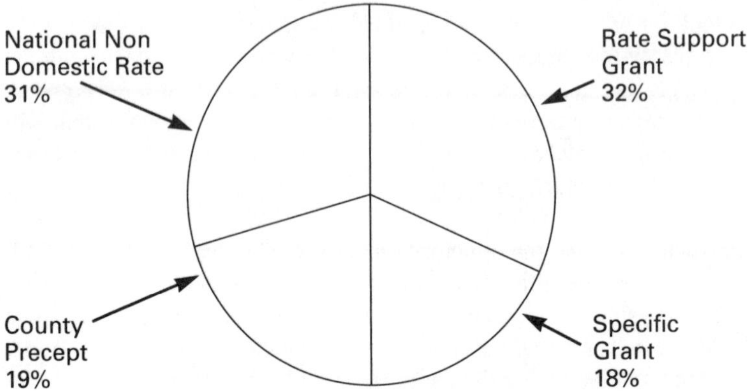

National Non
Domestic Rate
31%

Rate Support
Grant
32%

County
Precept
19%

Specific
Grant
18%

Chapter 4

The Personnel Manager and Management Information Systems

The environment in which organizations operate is so complex that it would be impossible for them to survive without detailed planning, monitoring and the use of information from a great variety of sources. It follows, therefore, that organizations must set up information systems that are helpful to management in running the operations for which they are responsible. This chapter looks at some of the financial information systems that are available to the Personnel Manager: they will be discussed in greater detail later in the book.

In planning it is necessary to have information, since no plan can be devised in a vacuum. The bulk of this information in most organizations is derived from actions that have taken place in the past. Management look at what has been happening over the last five years, with particular emphasis on the last year. Then, with the aid of economic forecasts and reports from their own sources, they attempt to decide what will happen to the organization over the next five or six years. It is extremely unlikely that any of these forecasts will be 100 per cent accurate even for the next year, but there is no doubt that the more information that is available the more accurate the forecast is likely to be.

Organizations that are new and making their forecasts for the first time are at something of a disadvantage in that they have no first-hand experience on which to draw. This does not mean that they should not attempt to plan—indeed, it is absolutely essential that they do, because organizations that do not plan fail. The lack of first-hand experience is a drawback, but there are normally other undertakings operating in the same field and much information can be obtained about them through publications such as 'Dunn and Bradstreet', as well as by spending money on market research. This will enable the new organization to prepare a fairly well-informed plan of activity at least for the next year, and as those responsible for planning within the organization gain experience their plans will improve.

Once the plan has been drawn up, it is essential that it is monitored continuously, so that differences between planned and actual performance can be readily seen, and corrective action taken where it is felt to be necessary. This can be achieved only if the relevant information is available at the right place and at the right time. One of the dangers of high technology is that those responsible for making decisions receive so much information that it is sometimes difficult to 'see the wood for the trees', and important things are overlooked. It is no use telling the Sales Manager the number of employees in the Production Department, or the Production Manager the cost of recruiting a Personnel Manager, at least not from the point of view of their decision making. Nor is it useful to tell a Production Manager at the end of August that he failed to meet his production target in January, as the information will be too late to be of any use at all. It is here that a good management information system is invaluable to any organization.

The Personnel Department has to work within organizational constraints and the overall plan, but the resources available to it will depend, to some extent, on the personality of the Personnel Manager. When the organizational budget is being prepared, each departmental manager will bid for the resources required for their department. The manager who is perceived to be providing good value for money and has prepared a strong case will, generally speaking, receive a larger share of the available resources than a less well-prepared and informed manager. It is therefore essential for the well-being of the Personnel Department, as well as for the organization as a whole, that the Personnel Manager is fully conversant with the system of budgetary control employed by the undertaking in which he or she is employed.

Having obtained an equitable share of the resources available it is incumbent upon the Personnel Manager to demonstrate that the organization is receiving good value from its investment. In order to achieve this each item of expenditure must be carefully measured against the best available alternative to demonstrate that expenditure is being incurred because it is needed and not simply because this is the way in which things have always been done. Methods of developing proposals have to be continually reviewed to see whether it might be better to buy in expertise rather than supply it internally, and it is now becoming more common for personnel departments to offer their training programmes in the open market as a way of obtaining additional income for training and development.

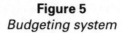

Figure 5
Budgeting system

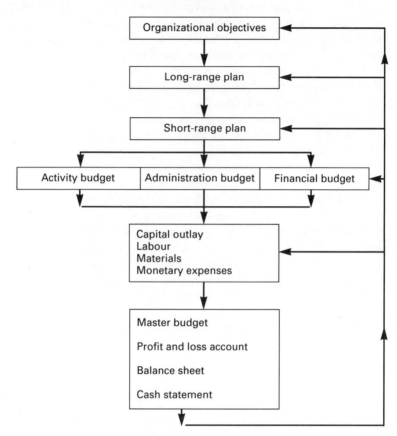

A system of budgeting is illustrated in figure 5, which demonstrates that there is feedback and control at every stage, and it is essential for the system to produce this information quickly and accurately. The budgetary system is an overall system of planning within an organization that ends in the master budget. This consists of statements of vital importance to organizational survival: the balance sheet, profit and loss account and cash statement, each of which will be discussed in this chapter and analysed in depth later in the book.

The balance sheet provides information on the position of an organization at a given date. It relates only to that date, since the position may vary significantly from day to day, which makes the date on which the balance sheet was prepared extremely important, as are the conventions that have been followed in drawing it up. Traditionally the balance sheet has been employed largely as an historical document, showing the organization's position at some point in the past and allowing relevant information to be derived from it.

There is no reason, however, why the balance sheet should not be used, as it is more often tending to be, as a planning document, to show what an organization will look like at some future date. The future position of the organization is of greater importance to those who are involved with it than what has happened in the past, although past lessons should never be forgotten.

The balance sheet is a specific sort of information system and its two-sided form is illustrated in example 1. This balance sheet, together with others, will be discussed in greater detail in chapter 4, but it can readily be seen that it could be used by the Personnel Manager to obtain information that might be helpful in counselling staff. The company, 'X Co.', has a liquidity problem. There is a bank overdraft of £10,000 and no cash available at all, which seems to make it very difficult for 'X Co.' to pay its way. This information could be useful, for example, when advising staff on their career plans. This and much more can be deduced when the balance sheet is correctly used in conjunction with ratios and other information, as will be demonstrated in chapter 4.

Example 1

Balance sheet of 'X Co.' as at 31 July

Fixed assets:			Capital	£100,000	
Land and			Reserves	90,000	
buildings	£180,000				190,000
Plant and					
machinery	90,000				
Motor vehicles	25,000		Loans		90,000
		295,000			
Current assets:			Current		
Stock	5,000		liabilities:		
Debtors	50,000		Creditors	40,000	
			Accruals	20,000	
			Bank		
			overdraft	10,000	
		55,000			70,000
		£350,000			£350,000

The profit and loss account, as its name suggests, gives information as to whether or not an organization, or part of it, is making a profit or loss. Like the balance sheet, it can be used either as an historical document or as a planning tool. It relates to a period of time, which may be a month, a quarter, a half-year, a year or any other period over which the organization wishes to measure the success or failure of its operations. The information that it provides will be altered by the conventions that have been followed in its preparation, particularly in the treatment of depreciation, research and development, and goodwill.

This account is divided into two parts, the first of which records the cost of the goods that have been sold, and compares it with the selling price to give the gross profit. The second part takes from the gross profit fixed costs like salaries, rates, depreciation, interest charges and stationery to arrive at the net profit.

The profit and loss account is illustrated in example 2, but it should be borne in mind that organizations which provide a service do not normally need to calculate a gross profit. The example shows a net profit of £15,000, but we do not yet have sufficient information to know whether that is good or bad; this and other points will be explained in chapter 5.

Example 2

Trading and profit and loss account of 'X Co.'
for the year ending 31 July

Sales		£300,000
Less cost of goods sold:		
Opening inventory	£ 5,000	
Add inventory purchased	180,000	
	185,000	
Less closing inventory	25,000	
Cost of inventory sold		160,000
Gross profit		140,000
Less Expenses:		
Wages and salaries	70,000	
Selling and distribution	20,000	
Heating and lighting	10,000	
Depreciation	5,000	
Financing charges	15,000	
Miscellaneous	5,000	
		125,000
Net profit		£ 15,000

The cash statement shows the cash position of an organization, and the balance appears in the balance sheet, either under the current assets as bank/cash in hand or under the current liabilities as bank/cash overdrawn at that date. The statement can be used either for historical reporting purposes or for planning and control, and is commonly utilized in both these ways. The information it contains is of vital importance to the survival of the organization as, without money, operations would have to cease. When used as a system of planning and control the cash statement is referred to as a cash budget and prepared on a daily, weekly, monthly or quarterly basis, and it is closely monitored, as described in chapters 6 and 13.

Example 3

Cash statement of 'X Co.' for the year ending 31 July

Opening cash in hand/(overdrawn)		£30,000
Receipts from cash sales	£ 50,000	
Receipts from credit sales	200,000	
		250,000
Total cash available		280,000
Less payments:		
Payments for cash purchases	100,000	
Payments for credit purchases	40,000	
Selling and distribution costs	20,000	
Heating and lighting	10,000	
Financing charges	15,000	
Miscellaneous costs	5,000	
Fixed assets purchased	100,000	
		290,000
Cash in hand/(overdrawn)		(£10,000)

This is one of the most important financial management information systems, and it is almost impossible to pay too much attention to this aspect of an organization. Example 3 shows a cash statement which indicates that the major reason for the overdraft of £10,000 is the capital expenditure of £100,000 on fixed assets during the year.

The Personnel Manager will be responsible for preparing the cash budget and monitoring the cash statement or his or her department. This control now normally takes place on a daily basis as it is essential for the Personnel Manager (and indeed the whole organization) to be constantly aware of the cash position and, where necessary, to react with the utmost speed. Many Chief Executives now insist that any surpluses are invested in the overnight market to make money.

Chapter 5

The Balance Sheet

The balance sheet is a statement that shows the position of the organization at a specific date, and like all statements its accuracy is dependent on the information system employed to compile it. If the information on which it is based is inaccurate the balance sheet will be inaccurate. This illustrates the central role of a good management information system in the effective running of an organization. In drawing up a balance sheet it is necessary to follow accounting conventions, which will be explored as we work through some illustrations.

Example 4

An entrepreneur has £20,000 with which to start a business and pays it into the business's bank account. The balance sheet would then show:

Business balance sheet
as at day 1

Uses		Sources	
Bank	£20,000	Capital	£20,000

The balance sheet shows that £20,000 has been put into the business by the owner and that at the time of the balance sheet it was all in the bank. Any resource put into a business by the owner(s) becomes part of the capital, and all sources of finance are shown on the right-hand side of the two-sided balance sheet. The uses of finance, including money in the bank, are shown on the left-hand side. Every balance sheet uses these principles, and if they are broken down item by item a great deal of the confusion that often surrounds them can readily be overome.

Example 5

Premises are required for the business, and enquiries lead to the purchase of a small lock-up shop for £18,000 on day 2. The shop is paid for and the balance sheet becomes:

Business balance sheet
as at day 2

Uses		Sources	
Premises	£18,000	Capital	£20,000
Bank	2,000		
	£20,000		£20,000

No new resources have been put into the business by the owner, nor have any been withdrawn, which leaves the capital unchanged; and, as no other resources have been provided, there is no change on the 'sources' side of the balance sheet. On the 'uses' side most of the money has been taken from the bank and invested in the premises, as reflected in the new balance sheet.

Example 6

The premises having been obtained, the business now requires inventory to sell in order to start trading. £1,000 of goods are purchased for cash on day 3. This transaction will be shown in the balance sheet as:

Business balance sheet
as at day 3

Uses		Sources	
Premises	£18,000	Capital	£20,000
Inventory/stock	1,000		
Bank	1,000		
	£20,000		£20,000

The sources side of the balance sheet remains unchanged but there has been a further change of use. £1,000 has been taken from the bank to purchase inventory, which is also referred to as stock, consisting of items held by the business for resale in order to earn a profit.

Example 7

Inventory that cost £100 is sold for £100 on day 6 to attract people into the shop. The balance sheet will then show:

Business balance sheet as at day 6

Uses		Sources	
Premises	£18,000	Capital	£20,000
Inventory/stock	900		
Bank	1,100		
	£20,000		£20,000

Once again the sources side of the balance sheet remains unchanged but the inventory is reduced by the £100 that has been sold and the bank increased by the £100 that has been received from the sale.

Example 8

On day 8 the business is really ready for action, and inventory that cost £800 is sold for £1,600 cash. The balance sheet will now show:

Business balance sheet as at day 8

Uses		Sources	
Premises	£18,000	Capital	£20,000
Inventory/stock	100	Reserves:	
Bank	2,700	Retained Profit	800
	£20,800		£20,800

The sources side of the balance sheet is increased by the profit on the sale of £800, which is shown under the reserves. This is balanced by the reduction in inventory of £800 and the increased bank balance of £1,600, which illustrates the fact that all the resources a business receives must be accounted for, whatever their nature, and explains why the balance sheet should always balance. The premises remain unchanged at £18,000

Example 9

The business is now in full stride and on day 9 further inventory is purchased for £3,000, of which £2,000 is in cash and £1,000 is credit.

Business balance sheet as at day 9

Uses		Sources	
Premises	£18,000	Capital	£20,000
Inventory/stock	3,100	Reserves:	
		Retained Profit	800
Bank	700	Creditor	1,000
	£21,800		£21,800

A new item appears on the sources side of the balance sheet, called creditor, of £1,000. Creditors are people who are owed money by the business for goods or services they have provided. This item is balanced by an increase of £3,000 in the inventory and a reduction in the bank balance of £2,000; no other changes take place in the balance sheet. It is interesting to note that the reserves are £800 but the bank balance is only £700. Reserves do not normally represent money!

Example 10

Business is booming. To encourage it, credit is offered to reliable customers, and on day 10 inventory that cost £1,800 is sold for £3,600. The sales consist of £600 for cash and £3,000 on credit. The balance sheet now shows:

Business balance sheet as at day 10

Uses		Sources	
Premises	£18,000	Capital	£20,000
Inventory	1,300	Reserves:	
Debtors	3,000	Retained Profit	2,600
Bank	1,300	Creditor	1,000
	£23,600		£23,600

The capital and creditor on the sources side remain unchanged, whilst the reserves are increased by the profit of £1,800 to £2,600, although the bank balance is only £1,300. Reserves do *not* represent cash. On the uses side, inventory is reduced by the £1,800 that has been sold, to £1,300, the bank balance is increased by the £600 received from the sale, to £1,300, and debtors of £3,000 for the credit sales appear. People who owe money to the business for goods or services received are called debtors.

Example 11

The business receives £1,200 that it is owed by some of its debtors and pays what is owed to its suppliers on day 11. The balance sheet will show:

Business balance sheet
as at day 11

Uses		Sources	
Premises	£18,000	Capital	£20,000
Inventory	1,300	Reserves:	
Debtors	1,800	Retained Profit	2,600
Bank	1,500	Creditor	
	£22,600		£22,600

The only change on the sources side is the disappearance of the creditor for £1,000 because payment has been made. On the uses side, the debtors are reduced by the £1,200 that they have paid and the bank balance is increased by £200 (£1,200 – £1,000); the premises and inventory remain unchanged.

You will have noticed that nothing that happens to a business can ever have only a single impact on the balance sheet. If this were not the case, the balance sheet would never balance and would serve no useful purpose. As has already been noted, the balance sheet, by its very nature, should always balance, and so each transaction that takes place must have more than one side to it. Transactions may have seven impacts or more but never just a single one, and this is the basis of the double-entry system of book-keeping that has been employed since the time of the Phoenicians. When we accountants see a good thing we know how to cherish it!

Some conventions have been followed in constructing the balance sheets, and these should be explained in a little more detail. The 'sources' and 'uses' sides are each arranged in order of permanence, with the most permanent item at the top and the least permanent at the bottom. The uses are divided into fixed, which are retained in the business to earn profits, like land and buildings, and current, which are consumed in order to earn profits, like inventory and money. The sources are allocated between permanent, consisting of capital and reserves, long term, consisting of loans, and current, which includes creditors. The balance sheet in example 10 takes the following form when these conventions are emphasized:

Example 10, Redrawn 1

Business balance sheet
as at day 10

Uses			*Sources*	
Fixed uses:			Capital	£20,000
Premises		£18,000	Reserves:	
Fixtures/fittings			Retained Profit	2,600
Motor vehicles			Loans	
			Current sources:	
Current uses:			Creditor	1,000
Inventory	£1,300			
Debtors	3,000			
Bank	1,300	5,600		
		£23,600		£23,600

These divisions between fixed and current uses and between permanent, long-term and current sources become important when we start to look at the interpretation of financial information.

Another convention that is normally followed is for sources to be called 'liabilities'. This is because everything on that side is technically held by the business on somebody else's behalf. The capital and reserves belong to the owner(s) of the business, the loans consist of money which belongs to the lenders, and creditors are the people who supplied the credit, so that everything on that side is a liability of the undertaking.

The uses are called 'assets' because they are owned by the business.

The premises, inventory and bank balance are all owned by the business, and the debtors are obliged to pay the business, so that their debt is owned by it. Using this new but more usually accepted terminology, the balance sheet becomes as follows.

Example 10, Redrawn 2

Business balance sheet
as at day 10

Assets			Liabilities	
Fixed uses:			Capital	£20,000
Premises	£18,000		Reserves:	
Fixtures/fittings			Retained Profit	2,600
Motor vehicles	_____	£18,000	Loans	
			Current liabilities:	
Current uses:			Creditors	1,000
Inventory	1,300		Accruals	
Debtors	3,000			
Bank	1,300	5,600		
		£23,600		£23,600

The fixtures and fittings and motor vehicles have been included as examples of fixed assets, the loans as an example of a long-term liability and accruals as a short-term liability, although nothing is yet shown against them. Accruals are sums due to be paid for items such as rent, rates and electricity.

The balance sheets that we have discussed so far have been in the two-sided form because they facilitate explanation, but most organizations publish their balance sheets in a vertical form, so we will redraw the above balance sheet in that form to illustrate the approach.

Example 10, Redrawn 3

Business balance sheet
as at day 10

Fixed assets:		
Premises	£18,000	
Fixtures and fittings		
Motor vehicles		£18,000
Current assets:		
Inventory	1,300	
Debtors	3,000	
Bank	1,300	
	5,600	
Less Current liabilities:		
Creditors	£1,000	
Accruals		
Net current assets (working capital)		4,600
Net assets employed (net capital employed)		£22,600
Financed by:		
Capital	20,000	
Reserves	2,600	
Owner's equity		
Loans		
		22,600
		£22,600

Organizations prefer to publish the balance sheet in the vertical (or, as it is sometimes called, the narrative) form because they believe it is easier for the lay person to understand than the two-sided form. Items that are considered to be important, like the net current assets (working capital) and net assets employed (net capital employed) are highlighted and can be further explored should the need arise. This will be further discussed in chapter 9 when we look at the interpretation of financial information.

When an organization turns itself into a limited company the major impact in the balance sheet is under the 'Capital' heading. If the business decided, through its formation documentation, that it would have the authority to issue 400,000 shares of 20p each and, in fact, issued 113,000 shares to the owner in return for the owner's equity, then the net assets employed (net capital employed) would be exactly as illustrated above, and total £22,600 but the 'Financed by' section becomes:

Financed by

Authorized capital:
400,000 shares of 20p each   £80,000

Issued capital:
113,000 shares of 20p each   £22,600
Reserves
Owner's equity
Loans
                                                              £22,600

The share capital of 113,000 shares of 20p has replaced the original owner's equity, which consisted of capital and reserves. This is to compensate the owner for the work that has to be carried out in starting up a business.

The following questions are for you to attempt before you check against the suggested answers provided below.

Exercise 1

Sacha has inherited £60,000 and intends to use it to fulfil a lifelong dream of setting up in business. On 5 June the money is paid into the business bank account. Draw up the balance sheet as at 5 June.

Exercise 2

On 6 June Sacha obtains premises for £80,000, of which £40,000 is paid from the business bank account by cash, and the other £40,000 is borrowed. Draw up the balance sheet as at 6 June.

Exercise 3

On 7 June fixtures and fittings of £8,000 are bought for cash. A small van that has been in Sacha's possession, worth £1,500 is brought into the business. Draw up the balance sheet as at 8 June.

Exercise 4

The business is now ready, so on 8 June Sacha buys inventory for £30,000, of which £20,000 is a credit purchase and the balance is paid in cash. Draw up the balance sheet as at 8 June.

Exercise 5

Sacha sells inventory that cost £20,000 for £60,000 on 9 June. £50,000 of the sales were on credit and the balance for cash. Draw up the balance sheet as at 9 June.

Exercise 6

The business is doing so well that on 10 June Sacha decides to turn it into a limited company, and issues 203,000 shares at 50p for the owner's equity. Draw up the balance sheet to show how it would appear after this transaction, in both the two-sided and vertical forms.

In every case the balance sheets show the position of the business at a particular date, and have been drawn up after the transactions have occurred, and so are used as historical documents. There is no reason why they should not be used as planning tools, showing the position it is planned for the business to be in at some specific future date. This will be further discussed in chapter 7.

Solution 1

Balance sheet of Sacha
as at 5 June

Assets		Liabilities	
Current assets:			
Bank	£60,000	Capital	£60,000

Solution 2

Balance sheet of Sacha
as at 6 June

Assets		Liabilities	
Fixed assets:		Capital	£60,000
Premises	£80,000	Loan	40,000
Current assets:			
Bank	20,000		
	£100,000		£100,000

It is assumed that the business borrowed the £40,000, and not Sacha. Had Sacha borrowed the money, then the capital would have become £100,000, with no loan appearing.

Solution 3

Balance sheet of Sacha
as at 7 June

Assets			Liabilities	
Fixed assets:			Capital	£61,500
Premises	£80,000		Loan	40,000
Fixtures/fittings	8,000			
Motor vehicle	1,500	£ 89,500		
Current assets:				
Bank		12,000		
		£101,500		£101,500

You can see that the capital has increased by £1,500. This is because the van that the owner has brought into the business becomes part of the capital, even though it has not been paid for. The bank balance is reduced by the £8,000 paid for the fixtures and fittings.

Solution 4

Balance sheet of Sacha
as at 8 June

Assets			Liabilities	
Fixed assets:				
Premises	£80,000			
Fixtures/fittings	8,000		Capital	£61,500
Motor vehicle	1,500	£ 89,500	Loan	40,000
Current assets:			Current liabilities:	
Inventory	30,000		Creditors	20,000
Bank	2,000	32,000		
		£121,500		£121,500

The creditors of £20,000 appear as a current liability, and the bank balance is reduced by the £10,000 paid, to £2,000. The inventory of £30,000 is a current asset.

Solution 5

Balance sheet of Sacha
as at 9 June

Assets			Liabilities	
Fixed assets:				
Premises	£80,000		Capital	£ 61,500
Fixtures/fittings	8,000		Reserves:	
Motor vehicle	1,500	£ 89,500	Retained	
			profit	40,000
			Loan	40,000
Current assets:			Current liabilities:	
Inventory	10,000		Creditors	20,000
Debtors	50,000			
Bank	12,000	72,000		
		£161,500		£161,500

The retained profit of £40,000 under 'reserves' on the liabilities side is the profit made on the sale. On the assets side the changes take place in the current assets section, where inventory is reduced by £20,000 to £10,000, the bank balance is increased by £10,000 to £12,000, and debtors for the credit sales of £50,000 appear.

Solution 6

Balance sheet of Sacha
as at 10 June

Assets			Liabilities	
Fixed assets:			Authorized and	
Premises	£80,000		issued share capital:	
Fixtures/fittings	8,000		203,000 shares	
Motor vehicle	1,500	£ 89,500	at 50p	£101,500
			Loan	40,000
			Current liabilities:	
Current assets:			Creditors	20,000
Inventory	10,000			
Debtors	50,000			
Bank	12,000	72,000		
		£161,500		£161,500

The capital and reserves have been replaced by the authorized and issued share capital. The vertical form of the balance sheet would be:

Balance sheet of Sacha
as at 10 June

Fixed assets:		
Premises	£80,000	
Fixtures and fittings	8,000	
Motor vehicle	1,500	
		£ 89,500
Current assets:		
Inventory	10,000	
Debtors	50,000	
Bank	12,000	
	72,000	
Less Current liabilities:		
Creditors	20,000	
Working capital		52,000
Net capital employed		£141,500
Financed by		
Authorized and issued share capital:		
203,000 shares at 50p each		101,500
Loan		40,000
		£141,500

We have worked together through a series of balance sheets and you have completed some exercises to give you a good understanding of the structure of the balance sheet. A more detailed interpretation of the information it contains (and its relevance to personnel managers) will appear in chapter 9, when the accounts of Marks & Spencer will be analysed.

Chapter 6

The Trading and Profit and Loss Account

We have seen from the previous chapter that it is possible to draw up a fresh balance sheet after every transaction that takes place in an organization, but with the number of transactions that take place, it would become extremely cumbersome to do so. In order to overcome the problem we have to devise some means of collecting together transactions that would be helpful to those who need the information as well as meaningful in financial terms. This is achieved through the trading and profit and loss account.

The balance sheet shows the position of the business at a planned future date or at a specific date in the past. The trading and profit and loss account (sometimes referred to as the income statement) shows the results of an organization's activities over a period of time which may be a week, a month, several months or a year, either as planned for, or as has occurred in the past. In preparing the trading and profit and loss account several accounting principles have to be observed.

Accounting principles

The matching principle

This ensures that each accounting period stands alone and collects all the earnings and expenses which relate to it. There is a danger that when transactions overlap two accounting periods they will be counted twice, once in each period, or missed altogether. The matching principle helps to avoid this.

For example, assume that the profit and loss account is drawn up for the year from 1 January to 31 December, and that business rates of £1,000 are paid on 1 October for the six months to 31 March. Then the three months until 31 December will belong in one profit and loss account and the three months until 31 March will belong in the next.

This is extremely important if the accounts are to be accurate enough to enable them to be used for purposes of comparison as well as recording the correct profit or loss.

A model of the organization through time would be like figure 6. If we did not have to manage the business, or pay taxes, or live, we would be able to wait until the end of its life before calculating the profit or loss that had been made. Unfortunately this is not possible, so each period's profit or loss has to be calculated. It is essential to ensure that all amounts which relate to that period are included and that any which relate to any other period are excluded. Achieving this happy result causes many problems in the preparation of financial information.

Figure 6
Organizational accounting through time

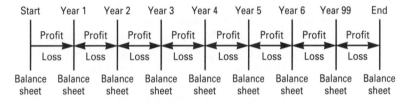

The principle of consistency

This helps in comparing performance in one financial period with that in another. If the methods employed when preparing the profit and loss accounts keep changing, comparison becomes impossible, so a decision must be made on how each item is to be dealt with. That method must continue to be used unless there is a very good reason for changing it.

An example is the way an organization treats the charge for the use of fixed assets in the profit and loss account. Because of their nature, most fixed assets are expensive and last a long time. It would be unfair if one accounting period were charged for the whole of the cost of a fixed asset and the other periods have free use of it. The period in which the asset was bought would show a loss and the other periods a profit, e.g.

Sales		£ 80,000
Cost of sales		20,000
Gross profit		60,000
Expenses	£ 40,000	
New fixed asset	100,000	
		140,000
Net loss		(£80,000)

In the next period, if the organization just happened to achieve exactly the same performance, the accounts would show:

Sales	£80,000
Cost of sales	20,000
Gross profit	60,000
Expenses	40,000
Net profit	£20,000

In order to avoid these wild fluctuations in profit we devise a means of charging a 'rent' for fixed assets, which we call depreciation. There are several ways of calculating the charge for depreciation. All are perfectly acceptable but the one that is most commonly used is the straight-line approach, which charges the same sum for the use of each asset over its life. To calculate the period charge for depreciation, three pieces of information are required—cost, life and scrap value.

If we have an asset that costs £101,000 which we estimate will last for ten years and have a residual scrap value of £1,000, then the charge for depreciation is given by:

$$\frac{\text{Cost} - \text{Scrap}}{\text{Life}} = \frac{£101,000 - £1,000}{10 \text{ years}}$$

$$= \frac{£100,000}{10 \text{ years}} = £10,000 \text{ p.a.}$$

This will make the profit in our example:

Sales		£80,000
Cost of sales		20,000
Gross profit		60,000
Expenses	£40,000	
Depreciation	10,000	50,000
Net profit		£10,000

This irons out the fluctuations in profit and facilitates comparison of performance.

The principle of conservatism

Accountants are by nature pessimistic. We feel it is better to look on the dark side and be surprised if things turn out better than expected, than to look on the bright side and be surprised if things turn out worse than expected. This is the principle of conservatism, under which we always anticipate losses but never profits. It is clearly demonstrated in the way in which inventory is valued.

Inventory is always valued at the lower of cost or current market value. If an item was purchased for £6,000 and its market value went up to £8,000 it would be valued in the accounts at £6,000. However, if its market value went down to £4,000 it would be valued in the accounts at £4,000.

The principle of differentiating between capital and revenue items

Capital transactions involve fixed assets and affect the balance sheet, so that if we buy new machinery it appears under fixed assets in the balance sheet and the bank balance is reduced by the same amount. There is at the time no impact on the profit and loss account, but there will be at some later date, through the charge for depreciation.

Revenue transactions relate to running expenses like heating and lighting, rent and rates, wages and salaries, which have a direct impact on the profit and loss account but no direct effect on the balance sheet. They will, however, later affect the retained profit under the reserves.

Profit

Having discussed the principles which are employed in the preparation of the trading and profit and loss account, let us see if we can decide what profit is and why it so often differs from cash. Profit may roughly be described as *the earnings of the period concerned, whether or not they have been received, minus the expenses of the same period, whether or not they have been paid.*

To take this a little further, profit may be illustrated as:

```
Sales
    Credit          £80,000
    Cash             20,000
                                    £100,000
Expenses
    Credit           10,000
    Cash             50,000
                                      60,000
    Profit                          £ 40,000
```

The earnings are £100,000 and the expenses £60,000, giving a profit of £40,000, but what has been the effect on the bank balance? The bank balance has not, as we might have expected, been increased by the profit of £40,000 but reduced by £30,000. This is because the actual amounts of money involved have been:

```
        Payments for expenses        £50,000
        Receipts from sales           20,000
        Net cash outflow             £30,000
```

The other transactions have involved credit, not cash. This shows that a profit of £40,000 has resulted in a cash reduction of £30,000, which highlights the important difference between profitability and liquidity, and helps to explain why so many profitable companies fail because they do not have the means to pay their way.

Let us look more closely at the trading and profit and loss account, using the illustration given in example 2 on page 17. The statement could have been prepared historically, say on 15 October, or it could have been devised as a planning document and prepared on 1 May. Whatever its purposes, the principles on which it is prepared are exactly the same. To reinforce the point we will go through the entries item by item.

Sales   £300,000

This figure represents the total sales for the year and it is included whether or not any money has been received. Money received late on account of last year's sales would be excluded from this year's figure.

Opening inventory   £5,000

This is the stock that was left over, unsold, at the end of the previous trading period. It is valued at cost or current market value, whichever is the lower.

Inventory purchased   £180,000

This is the total purchases of stock for the year and is included whether or not the money has been paid. Money paid late on account of last year's purchases would be excluded from the figure.

Closing inventory   £25,000

This is the stock that has not been sold, valued at the lower cost or current market value.

Wages and salaries   £70,000

This is the total that should have been paid during the year, taken from the wage records. Any wages that are due but unpaid would be included in this figure.

Selling and distribution   £20,000

This would include all the expenses that have been incurred during the year, whether they have been paid or not.

Heating and lighting   £10,000

This is the electricity, oil, gas, coal, etc., that has been consumed during the year. Some apportionment may be necessary to ensure that only the expenses that relate to the year are borne by that year. It can be obtained from accounts received and metered readings.

Depreciation   £5,000

This will be the charge decided upon for the use of the fixed assets, as described under the principle of consistency. It is purely an apportionment of expenses and has no effect on money.

Financing charges   £15,000

This will be the total of the costs incurred in raising loans and the interest paid. It does not include the repayment of loans, which is a balance-sheet item (a capital transaction).

Miscellaneous   £5,000

This will be the total of a whole series of sundry expenses, including telephone, postage, writing materials, refreshments and office cleaning.

Net profit   £15,000

This is the figure that, once it has been adjusted for things like taxation, will appear in the balance sheet under reserves.

Added value

So far we have discussed gross and net profit and you should have some understanding of the concepts involved. There is, however, an additional concept to which businesses and their owners attach great importance. This is 'added value', which illustrates how much an organization is able to add to the costs incurred when arriving at the selling price of a product. The concept has been developed to such an extent that it is one of the factors used when assessing the strength of a company.

Added value is calculated in the following way:

Sales turnover + other income = Gross income
Gross income – Bought-out costs = Added value
Added value – wage costs = Net profit before tax

Applying this to example 2, page 17, we have:

Sales turnover		£300,000
Less Materials	£160,000	
Selling	20,000	
Heating	10,000	
Finance	15,000	
Miscellaneous	5,000	
		210,000
Added value		£ 90,000

The added value then goes to meet wage costs and depreciation. If there is any left when these costs have been met it becomes profit.

The trading profit and loss account—and its relevance to the Personnel Manager as an aid to decision making—will be explored more fully in chapter 9, through the medium of the accounts of Marks & Spencer.

Chapter 7

The Cash Statement

Chapters 5 and 6 illustrated two financial statements: that which provides information about the position of a business at a given date, the balance sheet; and that which shows the results of a period of activity in terms of profit, the trading and profit and loss account (or income statement). This chapter concentrates on the cash statement, which shows what has happened to the money in the organization and relates to the bank/cash in hand or overdrawn figure in the balance sheet.

As is the case with the balance sheet and trading and profit and loss account, this statement can be prepared either for planning purposes or as an historical document, to show the results of past activities. When it is prepared for planning purposes on a daily, weekly or monthly basis the cash statement becomes the cash budget, which is dealt with in detail in chapter 13. In preparing the statement for past activities we have to concentrate on the movements of money rather than the transactions that have taken place. For example, the sales of £300,000 in example 2 on page 17 may consist of £200,000 cash and £100,000 credit, whilst £60,000 cash could have been received from credit sales in the previous year ending 31 July. Cash received would therefore be £260,000 and not the £300,000 shown as sales. We need to look at each entry in example 2 and arrive at its cash equivalent in order for the cash statement to be prepared. This will further emphasize the difference between profitability and liquidity.

Opening inventory. No cash movement.

Add *inventory purchased.* This depends on what has been paid. It could be that £150,000 was for cash and £30,000 on credit, but a further £50,000 could have been paid for previously purchased items so that the payment would be £200,000 (£150,000 + £50,000) and not the £180,000 shown.

Less closing inventory. No cash movement.

Wages and salaries. These would all be paid, £70,000.

Selling and distribution. There could be some outstanding payments, say £3,000, and £1,500 could have been paid for the previous year's outstanding, making the cash movement £18,500 (£20,000 − £3,000 + £1,500).

Heating and lighting. Some of these accounts could be waiting to be paid, say £4,000, and £3,000 relating to last year could have been paid. This would make the cash £9,000 (£10,000 − £4,000 + £3,000).

Depreciation. No cash movement. Depreciation is purely an apportionment of costs and does not increase them.

Financing charges. This depends on what has been paid. If they had all been paid, together with £3,000 from the previous year, the cash movement would be £18,000.

Miscellaneous. There is possibly £1,000 due to be paid for last year's expenses, making the cash movement £6,000.

There could well be other items that are not shown in this profit and loss account which would affect the cash balance. For example, the purchase of a new fixed asset, like machinery, for £80,000 would have a big impact, and had the owner drawn any money from the business for his or her own purposes that would have affected the cash but might well not have been included in salaries. If the owner is not paid a salary, then any money he or she draws is treated as if the owner were reclaiming some of the resources that were due from the business. On the other hand, if the owner is paid a salary for working in the business it is shown under salaries and not treated as drawings.

The historical cash statement drawn up on the above figures, assuming the opening balance was £2,000, is shown as example 12.

Example 12

Cash statement of X Co. for the year ending 31 July

Opening balance in hand/(overdrawn)	£2,000
Add receipts from cash sales	200,000
Add receipts from previous credit sales	60,000
Total cash available	262,000

Less cash payments:		
Goods purchased for cash	£150,000	
Add payments for previous credit purchases	50,000	
Wages and salaries	70,000	
Selling and distribution	18,500	
Heating and lighting	9,000	
Finance charges	18,000	
Miscellaneous	6,000	
		321,500
Closing cash in hand (overdrawn)		(£59,500)

The result of the activities has been a profit of £15,000. But at the same time there has been a cash outflow of £61,500 which, after deducting the opening balance of £2,000, leaves an overdraft of £59,500—once again emphasizing that profitability does not equal liquidity.

Bear in mind that no matter how large or small an organization is or whether it is in the public or the private sector, exactly the same principles are employed when the cash statement is prepared. The cash statement of a large manufacturing concern would include the items illustrated in example 13.

Example 13

	(£000)	(£000)
Opening balance	40	
Add receipts:		
Money from trading	40,000	
Investment receipts	100	
		40,140
Less payments:		
Raw materials	1,020	
Fuel and light	80	
Factory wages	22,144	
Administrative salaries	12,256	
Carriage outwards	250	
Business rate	2,300	
General office expenses	80	
Repairs	59	
Financing costs	121	
		38,310
Closing balance in hand		1,830

Individual departments within an organization can also have their own cash statements, since it is necessary for each manager to control his or her departmental cash situation. This is discussed in detail in chapter 16, but the statement of a typical personnel department would look something like example 14.

Example 14

Personnel Department Cash Statement

	(£000)	(£000)
Opening balance	20	
Share of organizational budget	180	
Externally provided training courses	90	
Inter-departmental training charges	40	
		330
Payments:		
Salaries	190	
Recruitment costs	60	
Training costs	60	
Heat and light	5	
Telephone, Postage	8	
Service charge	7	
		330
Balance		—

Do you feel that a balanced cash statement is the sign of a good personnel manager?

The following exercises relate to chapters 5–7 and are for you to attempt before comparing your answers with the suggested solutions that follow.

Exercise 7

Thomas has £5,000 with which to make a living and decides to become a market stall holder. He buys a pair of scales that cost £586, will last for an estimated six years and have a scrap value of £40, and a market stall on wheels that cost £1,140, will last an estimated four years and have a scrap value of £100. During his first four weeks' trading he buys second-grade fruit out of his original £5,000 for £2,600. At the end of the four weeks he has £3,800 left out of his takings after paying out:

Rent of yard	£120 (£40 per week)
Weekend help	180
Obstruction fines	140

At the end of the period he owes £40 rent and has fruit left unsold which cost £240. He considers half the fruit to be still saleable. Calculate the profit for the period, the cash statement, and the balance sheet at the end.

Exercise 8

At the start of his second four weeks' operations Thomas is in the following position:

Inventory of saleable fruit costing	£120
Cash in hand	4,474
One week's rent owing	40
A stall and a pair of scales	

In the second four weeks he buys £3,900 of fruit for cash. He decides, after consulting his accountant, that he should spend £400 on household expenses. He takes out a loss-of-profits insurance policy at the beginning of the period, payable in advance, at an annual premium of £208. Other cash transactions during the four weeks are:

Rent	£120 (three weeks)
Fines	260
Help	180
Cash takings	5,000

The closing value of inventory at cost is £500, half of which is in good condition and half of which he thinks will fetch only £150 (three-fifths of cost). What are his profit for the period, his cash balance and his financial position at the end of the second period? He finds he needs more to cover household costs. Can he afford it?

Exercise 9

Thomas's position at the start of the third four weeks is:

Two weeks' rent owing	£80
Insurance pre-paid	192
Inventory of fruit	400
Cash in hand	4,406
A pair of scales and the stall	

During the four weeks he buys fruit for £5,000 cash and feels that he can increase his household expenditure to £600. He does so and retains the balance of the money in the business. Other payments and receipts during the four weeks are:

Rent	£ 200 (five weeks)
Fines (one prosecution is pending.	
The fine is expected to be £300)	nil
Weekend help	180
Cash takings for the month	6,000

On the last day of the period he purchased a delivery van for £5,100 and sold his stall for £800. The value of his closing inventory was £600 at cost price. What was Thomas's profit for the period? Was there a profit or a loss on the sale of the stall? What was his financial position at the end of the period?

Exercise 10

Thomas starts his fourth four weeks with:

Cash in hand	£ 126
Provision for parking fine	300
Rent owing	40
Fruit unsold	600
Insurance pre-paid	176
Van	5,100
Scales	526

He senses that he is running into a cash-flow problem but his household costs are rising and so he increases the allocation to £650. The magistrates fine him £140 for the outstanding case of obstruction, and he decides to expand his business by starting a delivery round on the first day of the period, selling fresh vegetables with the fruit. He expects to keep the van for three years and then sell it for £810. His suppliers agree to let him open a credit account and the following transactions take place during the fourth four weeks:

Total cash purchases	£3,500
Total purchases on credit	3,000
Cash takings	6,100
Sales on credit to families whom he feels he can trust and who have promised to pay him next month	400
Inventory of fruit and vegetables at the end of the period at market value	1,700

His other cash transactions during the four weeks are:

Vehicle running expenses	£ 100
Annual vehicle licence	130
Rent paid	160
Weekend help	180
Payments to creditors	1,800

What is Thomas's profit for the period? What is his financial position at the end of the period? Does it accurately represent the worth of the business?

Solution 7

Trading and profit and loss account of Thomas for the first four weeks

Sales			£4,240
Less cost of goods sold:			
Opening inventory		£ 0	
Add inventory purchased		2,600	
		2,600	
Less closing inventory		120	
Cost of goods sold			2,480
Gross profit			1,760
Less Expenses:			
Rent of yard		£ 160	
Weekend help		180	
Obstruction fines		140	
Depreciation:			
Stall	20		
Scales	7	27	507
Net profit			£1,253

Cash statement

Opening balance			£5,000
Add money received from sales			4,240
			9,240
Less Payments:			
Rent of yard		£ 120	
Help		180	
Fines		140	
Scales		586	
Stall		1,140	
Fruit		2,600	
			4,766
Closing cash in hand			£4,474

Balance sheet of Thomas
as at the end of the first four weeks

Fixed assets:			Capital	£5,000
Scales	£ 586		Reserves:	
Less depreciation	7	£ 579	Retained profit	1,253
Stall	1,140			
Less depreciation	20	1,120		
		1,699		
Current assets:			Current liabilities:	
Inventory	120		Rent due	40
Cash	4,474			
		4,594		
		£6,293		£6,293

Although a profit of £1,253 has been earned, the cash balance has fallen from £5,000 to £4,474. This means that the business has not generated enough funds for its needs, mainly owing to the purchase of the fixed assets. The depreciation was calculated as follows:

Stall cost	£1,140
Less scrap	100
	£1,040

This is divided by life, which is four years, giving:

4×13 (which is the number of four-week periods in a year) = 52 periods.

We then have:

$$\frac{1040}{52} = £20 \text{ per four-week period}$$

Scales cost	£586
Less scrap	40
	£546

This is divided by life, which is six years, giving:

$$\frac{546}{(6 \times 13)} = \frac{546}{78} = £7 \text{ per four-week period}$$

The closing stock is valued at the lowest of cost or current market value. The rent of £160 is the rent that should be paid, i.e. four weeks at £40 per week, whether or not this is actually paid.

Solution 8

Trading and profit and loss account of Thomas for the second four weeks

Sales			£5,000
Less cost of goods sold:			
Opening inventory		£ 120	
Add inventory purchased		3,900	
		4,020	
Less closing inventory		400	
			3,620
Gross profit			1,380
Less Expenses:			
Rent		£ 160	
Fines		260	
Help		180	
Depreciation:			
Stall	£20		
Scales	7		
		27	
Insurance premium		16	
			643
Net profit			£ 737

Cash statement

Opening balance		£4,474
Add money received from sales		5,000
		9,474
Less Payments:		
Rent	£ 120	
Fines	260	
Help	180	
Household expenses	400	
Fruit	3,900	
Insurance	208	
		5,068
Closing cash in hand		£4,406

The insurance of £16 is given by taking one-thirteenth of the £208 paid.

Balance sheet of Thomas
as at the end of the second four weeks

Fixed assets:			Capital		
Scales	£ 586		Reserves:		£5,000
Less depreciation	14		Retained profit:		
		£ 572	First four weeks	£1,253	
Stall	1,140		Second four weeks	737	
Less depreciation	40			1,990	
		1,100			
Current assets:		1,672			
Insurance			Less household		
pre-paid	192		money (drawings)	400	
Inventory	400				
Cash	4,406		Current liabilities:		1,590
			Rent due		80
		4,998			
		£6,670			£6,670

A further profit of £737 has been made in the second four weeks but the cash balance has been reduced by £68, owing largely to the drawings and increased inventory. Generally it is bad to remove all the profit from a business, but £400 drawings seem reasonable out of a profit of £737, particularly as there is a large sum of money in the business.

Solution 9

Trading and profit and loss account of Thomas
for the third four weeks

Sales			£6,000
Less cost of goods sold:			
Opening inventory		£ 400	
Add purchases of fruit		5,000	
		5,400	
Less closing inventory		600	
			4,800
Gross profit			1,200
Less Expenses:			
Rent		£ 160	
Fines		300	
Help		180	
Depreciation:			
Stall	£20		
Scales	7		
		27	
Insurance		16	
			683
Net operating profit			517
Loss on sale of stall			280
Net profit			£ 237

The operating profit is the profit from normal business operations and excludes unusual or extraordinary items like the profit or loss on the sale of fixed assets. The accounting convention of anticipating losses has been followed by making a provision for the expected fine.

Sale of stall

Original cost of stall	£1,140
Less total depreciation (£20 × 3)	60
Book value of the stall	1,080
Proceeds of the sale	800
Loss on the sale	£280

Balance sheet of Thomas as at the end of the third four weeks

Fixed assets:			**Capital:**		£5,000
Van		£5,100	Reserves:		
Scales	£586		Retained profit		
Less depreciation	21		First four weeks	£1,253	
		565	Second four weeks	737	
			Third four weeks	237	
				2,227	
			Less drawings		
			Second four weeks	£400	
			Third four weeks	£600	
				1,000	1,227
Current assets:			**Current liabilities:**		
Insurance pre-paid	176		Rent due	40	
Inventory	600		Fine pending	300	
Cash	126				340
	902				
	£6,567				£6,567

Cash statement

Opening balance		£4,406
Add sales receipts		6,000
Receipt from sale of stall		800
		11,206
Less payments:		
Delivery van	£5,100	
Fruit	5,000	
Household expenses	600	
Rent	200	
Help	180	
		11,080
Closing cash in hand		£ 126

A further operating profit of £517 has seen the cash balance reduced to £126 because of the purchase of the delivery van. Thomas will have to go through a period of consolidation if he is to stabilize his cash situation.

Solution 10

Trading and profit and loss account of Thomas for the fourth four weeks

Sales			£6,500
Less cost of goods sold:			
Opening inventory		£ 600	
Add purchases of fruit and vegetables		6,500	
		7,100	
Less closing inventory		1,700	
			5,400
Gross profit			1,100
Add overprovision for fine recovered:			160
Less expenses:			
Rent		160	
Help		180	
Vehicle running		100	
Vehicle licence		10	
Insurance		16	
Depreciation:			
Vehicle	£110		
Scales	7	117	
			583
Net profit			£ 677

The vehicle licence of £10 is calculated by taking one-thirteenth of £130.

Cash statement

Opening balance		£ 126
Add sales receipts		6,100
		6,226
Less payments:		
Inventory purchased for cash	£3,500	
Payments to creditor for inventory	1,800	
Vehicle running expenses paid	100	
Vehicle licence purchased	130	
Rent	160	
Help	180	
Household expenses	650	
Fine	140	
		6,660
Cash overdrawn		(£434)

Balance sheet of Thomas as at the end of the fourth four weeks

Fixed assets:					Capital			£5,000
Vehicle	£5,100				Reserves:			
Less depreciation	110		4,990		First four weeks	£1,253		
					Second four weeks	737		
Scales	586				Third four weeks	237		
Less depreciation	28		558		Fourth four weeks	677	2,904	
					Less drawings			
					Second four weeks	400		
					Third four weeks	600		
					Fourth four weeks	650	1,650	1,254
Current assets:								
Insurance pre-paid	160				Current liabilities:			
Inventory	1,700				Rent due	40		
Licence	120				Creditor	1,200		
Debtors	400		2,380		Bank overdraft	434		1,674
			£7,928					£7,928

Thomas's profit is £677. The balance sheet shows his financial position at the end of the fourth four weeks, but only on the assumption that the business is going to continue. If he were to close the business and sell his assets a very different picture could emerge. For example, the vehicle might realize £3,000 instead of the £4,990 shown in the books, and the scales £40 instead of the book value of £558. There is a problem with liquidity and Thomas may temporarily have to reduce spending on the family.

Chapter 8

The Manufacturing Account

Organizations that manufacture their own goods for sale require an additional financial statement to provide information on the cost of the goods that are being made. This helps to ensure that the manufacturing manager is able to maintain control over his or her operation and that the correct information is provided to facilitate good decision making. The manufacturing account comes before the trading and profit and loss account, and collects together all the costs of manufacture. These are transferred to the trading and profit and loss account in the 'cost of goods sold' section, where it replaces 'inventory purchased'. We shall explore this more fully as we work through example 16, but it is important to remember that the manufacturing account is part of the management information system and can either be prepared historically or used as a planning tool.

Example 15

Manufacturing account of Makes Co. for the year ending 30 June

Opening inventory of raw materials		£40,000
Add raw materials purchased		810,000
		850,000
Less closing inventory of raw materials		60,000
Raw materials consumed		790,000
Direct manufacturing wages		1,410,000
Direct expenses		10,000
Prime/direct cost of goods made		2,210,000
Add indirect factory expenses/overheads		
Salaries and wages	£70,000	
Materials	30,000	
Heating and lighting	40,000	
Rent and rates	60,000	
Depreciation	90,000	
		290,000
Total manufacturing costs		2,500,000
Add opening work in progress		10,000
		2,510,000
Less closing work in progress		20,000
Cost of finished goods made		£2,490,000

Example 15 shows a manufacturing account, which contains useful information for management. It can be made even more useful if it is broken down into the cost per unit produced, as we will see in chapter 10. The way in which the manufacturing account fits in with the trading and profit and loss accounts will be developed later, but in order to clarify the situation, let us first look at each item in the manufacturing account in turn.

Opening stock of raw materials. The raw materials that are available to be used at the beginning of the financial period. They are valued at the lower of cost or current market value.

Raw materials purchased. The raw materials purchased during the financial period under review. They need not necessarily have been paid for.

Closing stock of raw materials. The raw materials that are left unused at the end of the financial period. They become the opening stock of raw materials for the new period and are valued at the lower of cost or current market value.

Raw materials consumed. The raw materials that have actually been used in the manufacturing process.

Direct manufacturing wages. The wages of the people who are directly involved in making the product. It includes the machine operators but excludes supervisors and packers.

Direct expenses. Expenses that can be identified with a particular product, and which increase as the number of units produced increases. An example would be power metered separately to a machine making a single product. There are often no direct expenses in a manufacturing concern.

Indirect factory expenses/overheads. Expenses that are not identified with a particular product and generally remain fixed irrespective of the number of items produced. It is often difficult to arrive at the total to be charged to the manufacturing account, as opposed to the trading and profit and loss account. For example, a small manufacturing concern may have one rates bill for the whole site, and then have to apportion it between the manufacturing and non-manufacturing areas.

Salaries and wages. The remuneration paid to the factory manager, supervisors, cleaners and others whose time is spent in the manufacturing area.

Materials. The cost of materials used in the area that do not go directly into the product. They include such things as cleaning materials, packaging and general-issue items like screws.

Heating and lighting. The cost of heating and lighting the factory or workshop area. If there is one bill for the whole premises, some apportionment between the manufacturing and non-manufacturing areas will be necessary.

Rent and rates. The cost of rent and rates relating to the factory or workshop. Some apportionment will be necessary between the manufacturing and non-manufacturing areas if they are not billed separately.

Depreciation. The charge for the use of machinery, equipment, buildings and other fixed assets in the manufacturing area.

Total manufacturing costs. The total cost, collected together in the manufacturing account, of all the items that have been produced.

The relationship of the manufacturing account to the trading and profit and loss accounts can be illustrated as follows:

Example 16

Trading and profit and loss account of Makes Co. for the year ending 30 June

Sales		£7,600,000
Less cost of goods sold:		
Opening inventory of finished goods	£ 40,000	
Add cost of goods manufactured	2,490,000	
	2,530,000	
Deduct closing inventory of finished goods	30,000	
Cost of finished goods sold		2,500,000
Gross profit		£5,100,000

This is the end of the trading account. We then go on to the profit and loss account section:

Gross profit		£5,100,000
Less Expenses:		
Wages and Salaries	£3,750,000	
Selling and distribution	250,000	
Heating and lighting	40,000	
Depreciation	120,000	
Financing charges	65,000	
Miscellaneous	15,000	
		4,240,000
Net profit before tax		£ 860,000

There would then be deductions for tax but the amount would depend on the current tax legislation, which changes every year, and is therefore beyond the scope of this book.

The manufacturing account is used to ensure that the costs of manufacturing are properly controlled and that wastage is kept to a minimum. Correctly and promptly prepared accounts ensure that management is fully conversant with the current situation and able to take corrective action quickly when it proves to be necessary. If, for example, the Production Manager has evidence that raw material costs are escalating because of theft, she or he would liaise with the Personnel Manager to ensure that the correct procedures were being followed.

It may be that the organization finds that the demand for its manufactured product is price-sensitive and that a competitor is selling an equivalent item more cheaply. This will cause market share to be lost so that management will have to decide on how to combat the threat. The manufacturing account should provide sufficient detail for the cost of each item manufactured to be calculated. Comparison with the competitive selling price of the product will indicate to the management the courses of action that are open to it. Where the competitor's price is higher than the manufacturing cost it might be possible to reduce the selling price in order to reclaim lost market share. If, on the other hand the manufacturing cost is higher than the competitor's selling price then management has a major problem to resolve.

The selling price could be reduced below the cost price in the hope of recovering market share and possibly forcing the competitor out of business, but this is an extremely high-risk strategy and could not be pursued for a long period unless the organization is financially strong. A second option would be to investigate ways of reducing manufacturing costs so that the selling price could be brought down.

The Personnel Manager might well be closely involved in this process since a common way of controlling costs is by reducing staff numbers and counselling is often provided to those made redundant. In the event that neither of these strategies proves possible, a search would be made for a new product or products into which it might be worth diversifying. The last resort would be to endeavour to sell the organization as a going concern before it was forced into liquidation.

Example 15 shows that the cost of goods made was £2,490,000. If that cost was for manufacturing 800,000 units then the cost per unit would be:

$$£2,490,000 \div 800,000 = £3.11$$

A competitor coming to the market with a similar product selling at £10 would not, under normal circumstances, present a major threat. On the other hand one coming into the market at £5 would be a major problem, particularly as the product is at present selling for £9.46 (assuming sales of 803,215 units to achieve the sales value of £7,600,000 shown in the accounts).

Chapter 9

The Interpretation and Use of Financial Information

In the preceding chapters we have investigated the financial information that is provided by the management information system and noted the danger of information being received too late to be useful. Assuming that the organization has ensured that the correct information is reaching the right person quickly enough to be useful, we will look at some of the ratios that will help people make better use of the information in planning and control.

The ratios breakdown into three main areas: profitability, liquidity and efficiency. We will investigate each in turn, using the accounts of 'Trader Co'.

Example 17

Trading and profit and loss account of Trader Co. for the year ending 31 August

Sales		£960,000
Less cost of goods sold:		
Opening inventory of finished goods	£ 12,000	
Add finished goods purchased	488,000	
	500,000	
Less closing inventory of finished goods	30,000	
Cost of finished inventory sold		470,000
Gross profit		490,000
Less expenses:		
Wages and salaries	150,000	
Selling and distribution	75,000	
Heating and lighting	45,000	
Depreciation	70,000	
Financing charges	35,000	
Miscellaneous	15,000	
		390,000
Net profit		£100,000

Balance sheet of Trader Co. as at 31 August

Fixed assets:			Capital		£4,600,000
Land and buildings		£4,050,000	Reserves:		
Plant and machinery	£3,864,000		retained profit		875,000
Less depreciation	1,800,000	2,064,000	Loan		1,725,000
Fixtures and fittings	1,266,000				
Less depreciation	200,000	1,066,000			
Motor vehicles	65,000				
Less depreciation	45,000	20,000			
		7,200,000	Current liabilities:		
Current assets:			Creditors	£40,000	
Inventory	30,000		Accruals	10,000	
Debtors	20,000				50,000
Bank	0				
		50,000			
		£7,250,000			£7,250,000

Profitability ratios

These are concerned with the return on the long-term investment in the organization, that is, the return on the capital employed; and with the return on the sales, showing how much the sales contribute to fixed costs (those that do not change with the level of activity, like salaries) and whether there is enough left over for a profit, make useful control ratios.

We will look first at the return on the capital employed. The most accepted measure of capital employed is the 'net capital employed', which is the total assets minus the current liabilities.

Gross profit as a percentage of the net capital employed

This is calculated using the formula:

$$\frac{\text{Gross profit} \times 100}{\text{Net capital employed}} = \frac{\pounds490,000 \times 100}{(\pounds7,250,000 - \pounds50,000)}$$

$$= \frac{\pounds49,000,000}{\pounds7,200,000} = 6 \cdot 8\%$$

This figure in isolation is of little or no value, but if a trend over five years is obtained we can see whether management is able to exercise control over the organization's operations. In this example the gross profit is largely dependent on the difference between the buying price and the selling price, and once a figure has been accepted as reasonable for the gross profit as a percentage of the net capital employed it should not alter significantly unless the management decides that it should. If a return of 6·7 per cent is considered acceptable and over five years the actual results have been 6·6 per cent, 6·7 per cent, 6·7 per cent, 6·8 per cent, then analysts would be happy that, at least with regard to the buying and selling of goods, the organization was operating satisfactorily. On the other hand, a set of results showing 6·0 per cent, 7·2 per cent, 5·8 per cent, 6·3 per cent and 7·0 per cent would leave a serious question mark over the organization's management.

Whenever performance is being measured it should be remembered that one figure in isolation is useless. Only a set of results showing a trend over five years or so can be meaningful, and the average for the industry or business sector, which can be found in publications like 'Dunn and Bradstreet', would be helpful.

Net profit as a percentage of the net capital employed

This is calculated using the formula:

$$\frac{\text{Net profit} \times 100}{\text{Net capital employed}} = \frac{£100,000 \times 100}{(£7,250,000 - £50,000)}$$

$$= \frac{£10,000,000}{£7,200,000} = 1 \cdot 4\%$$

This figure shows the overall return on the long-term investment in the business and can be compared with the return that could be earned from investing the money safely in a bank, building society or national savings. Clearly 1·4 per cent is far less than could be earned almost anywhere else with the money. Using this criterion, the result for the year is poor. To discover whether it is a freak result we need the average for the last five years as well as the average for the business sector in which the concern operates. If it is a true representation of the return the organization makes, then in purely financial terms the organization should be closed down and the money invested where it would earn a higher return. There may, however, be good reasons for remaining in business. The organization might be providing a valuable service, or the owners may enjoy what they are doing so much that they do not wish to close. It is always dangerous to make decisions on limited information, but ratios do highlight areas that require investigation.

Gross profit as a percentage of sales

This is calculated using the formula:

$$\frac{\text{Gross profit} \times 100}{\text{Sales}} = \frac{£490,000 \times 100}{£960,000} = 51\%$$

This figure is a useful control ratio, as it represents the difference between the buying price and the selling price of the goods and, once it has been decided upon, should not alter from period to period. Again, it is of little use in isolation, but a trend over five or more years will reveal much about the way in which the organization is being controlled. The gross profit as a percentage of sales is a reflection of the mark-up, the amount that has been added to the cost price of the goods to arrive at the selling price. The calculation of the mark-up is (selling price – cost price) as a percentage of the cost price, which in this example is:

$$\frac{(£960,000 - £470,000) \times 100}{£470,000} = \frac{£490,000 \times 100}{£470,000} = 104 \cdot 3\%$$

This is to say that the organization is adding 104·3 per cent to the cost price of the goods to arrive at the selling price. This may sound a lot, but it should be remembered that all the running costs of the organization as well as the profit have to be met out of this figure.

Net profit as a percentage of sales

This is calculated using the formula:

$$\frac{\text{Net profit} \times 100}{\text{Sales}} = \frac{£100,000 \times 100}{£960,000} = 10 \cdot 4\%$$

This represents the percentage of sales that is left over for profit once all the other expenses have been met. When compared with the average for the industry and a trend over five or more years it is possible to see whether the organization is performing better or worse than average, and whether it is improving or deteriorating with time. In common with all ratios, the one does not provide a definitive answer but indicates where it may be necessary to investigate further. Even activities like recruitment and training are inextricably linked in with profitability ratios (hence the need for the Personnel Manager to understand them and always keep in mind the position of the business). After all, when an organization is failing to make good use of its resources there is little point in recruiting additional people who may shortly have to be released. And staff who require training often need help defining their needs, which always depend on the likely future direction of the whole business.

Liquidity ratios

These are concerned with an organization's ability to pay its way in the medium and short term. Like all other ratios, they do not indicate much about the organization when taken on their own, but used in conjunction with the average for the sector and the trend over the last five or more years they become good indicators of overall liquidity.

Current ratio

This is given by current assets as a ratio of current liabilities, with the current liabilities represented as unity (1). In our example we have current assets of £50,000 and current liabilities of £50,000. To express this as a ratio, we have current assets : current liabilities, and this becomes £50,000 : £50,000. Since the current liabilities are always shown as 1, to arrive at the figure for the current assets we divide the current assets by the current liabilities:

$$\frac{\text{Current assets}}{\text{Current liabilities}} = \frac{£50,000}{£50,000} = 1$$

So we have the current ratio of 1 : 1.

This indicates the organization's ability to pay its way in the medium term, that is, about four to nine months into the future. We can see that the current assets just cover the current liabilities but we have no indication of whether that is good or bad. Some organizations, like Williams Holdings in the retail sector, for example, have a current ratio of 2·7 : 1, whereas Tesco Stores has a current ratio of 1·3 : 1, so it is important to know the average for the sector and the trend for this ratio, where changes may be far more important than the actual figure.

Quick ratio (acid test)

This is given by the quick assets as a ratio of the current liabilities. The 'quick' assets are those that can readily be turned into cash. These obviously exclude fixed assets and normally also exclude the figure for inventory. In the example we have quick assets of £20,000 and current liabilities of £50,000, giving a quick ratio or acid test of:

$$20,000 : 50,000 = \frac{£20,000}{£50,000} : 1$$

$$= 0·4 : 1$$

This seems an extremely low ratio, but when compared with such companies as Sainsbury's and Tesco, which run on low quick ratios of approximately 0·2 : 1, it appears less of a problem.

Looking at the balance sheet, we see that there is no money and that there are relatively low debtors of £20,000 against creditors of £40,000. Much depends on how quickly inventory can be turned into money, and it would be interesting to see the trend over the last five or more years, but certainly alarm signals are flashing and further investigation is required into the short-term liquidity of the Trader Co.

The long-term solvency ratio and gearing

The long-term solvency ratio, often referred to in the UK as the gearing ratio and in America as the leverage, is of great importance to Personnel Managers and others. The higher the gearing, that is to say the greater the borrowing as a proportion of the total long-term financing, the higher the risk of business failure. This is due to the fact that money is a valuable asset that has to be paid for through interest – the more the borrowing, the greater the amount of money that has to be found. This can lead to cash-flow problems when profits fall and even possible business failure. Management should borrow enough to benefit the business but not so much as to cause problems; it is here that the gearing ratio can be helpful. If your organization's gearing ratio is below the average for the business sector, no major problems should ensue. On the other hand, if it goes above the average, alarms should sound and pertinent questions should be asked.

Efficiency ratios

Efficiency ratios indicate how effectively the inventory, creditors and debtors of the organization are being managed. These latter all form part of the working capital, which, remember, is current assets minus current liabilities. Lack of working capital means that the organization cannot be run effectively, so it has to be carefully managed. There are three efficiency ratios that will be considered.

Rate of inventory turnover, or age of inventory

This tells the organization how many times the inventory is changed in a year, or how long on average it is held before being used. The objective of most organizations is to hold as little inventory as possible for as short a time as possible. The advent of the 'just in time' system of inventory management is an attempt to hold no inventory at all but to buy stock as it is needed. This is proving extremely difficult to achieve in practice but there is certainly a strong move towards it. Money tied up in inventory is regarded by many as dead money that could be put to better use elsewhere.

In calculating the speed with which inventory is being used we employ the formula: cost of inventory used divided by the year-end inventory or, where there is sufficient information, the average inventory holding during the period under review. A rough average inventory holding is given by:

$$\frac{\text{Opening inventory} + \text{Closing inventory}}{2}$$

Trader Co. has opening inventory of £12,000 and closing inventory of £30,000, which gives an average inventory of:

$$\frac{£12,000 + £30,000}{2} = \frac{£42,000}{2} = £21,000$$

The cost of inventory used is cost of finished inventory sold, £470,000, so the number of times the inventory has been turned over is given by dividing £470,000 by £21,000, i.e. 22 times a year. It is therefore held on average for:

$$\frac{52}{22} : 2 \cdot 4 \text{ weeks}$$

This would be regarded as quite fast for most organizations, but a petrol retailer or fast-food shop would be very unhappy with it, so again we need to look at the average for the sector and the trend over the last five or more years before we can begin to draw any conclusions.

Speed of turnover of creditors, or age of creditors

This indicates how many times the creditors are turned over (not physically!) in the year, or how many weeks they are kept waiting for their money. Most organizations try to ensure that they are not paying their suppliers any more quickly than they receive money from their customers.

In calculating the speed with which we pay our suppliers we apply the formula: credit purchases (if the credit purchases are not known the total purchases figure is used) divided by the year-end creditors. Using the figures in our example, we have £488,000 divided by £40,000, i.e. 12 per year. This shows that on average they have had to wait 52/12 = 4·3 weeks for their money. This is very quick by today's standards. Most organizations keep their suppliers waiting more than 4·3 weeks, but once again the figure should be treated with care and should be compared with the trend over five or more years, the industry average and the speed with which money is collected from customers.

Speed of turnover of debtors, or age of debtors

This indicates the number of times the debtors are turned over in the year, or how many weeks they take to pay for the goods they have received from the organization. The formula used is credit sales (if known, otherwise the total sales figure is used) divided by the year-end debtors. Using the figures in our example, we have £960,000 divided by £20,000. This means we have collected money from our customers approximately 48 times in 52 weeks, showing that on average the organization has had to wait approximately one week for its money. (Using the alternative convention of working in days and assuming 360 working days in a year, 360/48 = 7·5 days, which again indicates that virtually all the sales are converted into cash in one week.)

We can now investigate the quick ratio or acid test further in the light of this new information. The acid test was 0·4 : 1, which appeared to indicate short-term liquidity problems, but we now know that sales are converted into cash within a week, and suppliers are kept waiting four weeks for their money. Assuming sales take place evenly throughout the year, the daily value of goods sold is:

$$\frac{£960,000}{360} = £2,667$$

In other words, the creditors of £40,000 could be paid from fifteen days of sales, so what at first sight appears to be a serious liquidity problem turns out to be more manageable when additional information is available.

The liquidity and efficiency ratios are key indicators that enable management to ensure that the organization will survive and is successfully meeting the operating targets. Since the Personnel Manager is often an important member of the executive team, present at meetings where critical decisions are made, a good knowledge of the financial ratios is essential if he or she is to contribute fully to the discussion.

Exercise 11

Apply these ratios where possible to exercises 7–10 at the end of chapter 7 and state whether you feel things are improving or deteriorating. Then compare your answers with the suggested ones given below.

73

Solution 11

Thomas's ratios

Period 1	*Period 2*	*Period 3*	*Period 4*

Net profit as a percentage of the net capital employed

$$\frac{\text{Net profit} \times 100}{\text{Net capital employed}}$$

$$\frac{£1,253 \times 100}{£6,253} = 20\% \qquad \frac{£737 \times 100}{£6,590} = 11 \cdot 2\% \qquad \frac{£237 \times 100}{£6,227} = 3 \cdot 8\% \qquad \frac{£677 \times 100}{£6,254} = 10 \cdot 8\%$$

Gross profit as a percentage of the net capital employed

$$\frac{\text{Gross profit} \times 100}{\text{Net capital employed}}$$

$$\frac{£1,760 \times 100}{£6,253} = 28 \cdot 1\% \qquad \frac{£1,380 \times 100}{£6,590} = 20 \cdot 9\% \qquad \frac{£1,200 \times 100}{£6,227} = 19 \cdot 3\% \qquad \frac{£1,100 \times 100}{£6,254} = 17 \cdot 6\%$$

Period 1	*Period 2*	*Period 3*	*Period 4*

Mark-up

$$\frac{(\text{Selling price} - \text{Cost price}) \times 100}{\text{Cost price}}$$

Period 1	*Period 2*	*Period 3*	*Period 4*
$\dfrac{£1,760 \times 100}{£2,480} = 71\%$	$\dfrac{£1,380 \times 100}{£3,620} = 38.1\%$	$\dfrac{£1,200 \times 100}{£4,800} = 25\%$	$\dfrac{£1,100 \times 100}{£5,400} = 20{\cdot}4\%$

Current ratio

Current assets : current liabilities

Period 1	*Period 2*	*Period 3*	*Period 4*
£4,594 : £40 = 114·8 : 1	£4,998 : £80 = 62.5 : 1	£902 : £340 = 2.7 : 1	£2,380 : £1,674 = 1·4 : 1

Quick ratio (acid test)

Quick assets : current liabilities

Period 1	*Period 2*	*Period 3*	*Period 4*
£4,474 : £40 = 111.9 : 1	£4,598 : £80 = 57·5 : 1	£302 : £340 = 0.89 : 1	£680 : £1,674 = 0·4 : 1

Period 1	Period 2	Period 3	Period 4

Rate of inventory turnover

$$\frac{\text{Cost of inventory sold}}{\text{Average inventory}}$$

Period 1	Period 2	Period 3	Period 4
$\dfrac{£2,480}{£120} = 20 \cdot 7$ times	$\dfrac{£3,620}{£260} = 13 \cdot 9$ times	$\dfrac{£4,800}{£500} = 9 \cdot 6$ times	$\dfrac{£5,400}{£1,150} = 4 \cdot 7$ times

Age of debtors: Not meaningful in this example

Age of creditors: Not meaningful in this example

We have considered the ratios of fictitious organizations and seen how they are calculated. It is important for personnel managers to understand them and their purpose so that they can use them to reinforce any points that they may wish to make either in discussions with individuals or in meetings. Let us now apply what we have learned to the accounts of a highly respected organization renowned for its excellent employee relations – Marks and Spencer.

MARKS AND SPENCER PLC
Report of the Directors

FINANCE
Accounting developments
Our financial statements for the year have been presented in accordance with FRS3 'Reporting Financial Performance'. Although we are not required to report under this standard until next year, early compliance is encouraged by the Accounting Standards Board (ASB) and we have adopted it this year.

The main presentational changes introduced by FRS3 are a new format for the Profit and Loss account and a new primary 'Statement of Total Recognised Gains and Losses'.

The Standard requires that turnover down to operating profit in the Profit and Loss account is split between continuing and discontinued activities. Our action taken last year to materially curtail our presence in Canada by downsizing the M&S division and disposing of Peoples, is treated as discontinued. The 1992 comparative figures have been restated to include a full year's turnover and operating profits for these discontinued activities. As published, the 1992 accounts only included turnover and profit up to November 1991 when the decision to reduce our Canadian operations was made. The remaining four months' results were included in the exceptional and extraordinary charges in accordance with the existing rules at that time.

Last year, we disclosed an extraordinary charge of £29·8m representing the loss on disposal of Peoples. As required by FRS3, this is now shown as an exceptional item. As a result, the 1992 published profit before tax of £623·5m and earnings per share of 14·8p have been restated.

Cash flow
The consolidated cash flow statement on page 32 shows how we have generated significant 'free' cash this year after substantial tax and dividend payments and capital expenditure of £255m.

A net cash inflow of £129m before financing and treasury activities has resulted in a marked decrease in net group borrowings. Consequently, gearing is now 4.2% compared with 9.8% last year as restated.

Net interest income rose to £22m from £11m last year as a result of the increase in sterling cash balances, although this was partly offset by lower UK interest rates and the impact of a weaker pound on the cost of our overseas borrowings.

Treasury policy
The Group's Treasury provides a service to the UK retail and financial services operations and overseas businesses, seeking to add value within clearly defined and narrow limits. Investment of the Group's cash is made within policies to control security, liquidity and rates achieved.

Borrowing for financial activities is arranged to match the nature of the related underlying assets. Overseas borrowing is arranged in the currencies in which subsidiaries operate.

Property valuation
The ASB has recently issued two discussion papers concerning the valuation of fixed assets. These argue in favour of showing assets in financial statements at up-to-date valuations rather than at historic cost. We will respond to the ASB with the object of arriving at valuation methods which accurately reflect the value of our UK stores as generators of retail profits irrespective of the state of the property market.

1993/94
Next year's accounting period will incorporate a 53rd week. This periodic adjustment is necessary so that we can continue to report to a 31 March year end.

The directors have pleasure in submitting their report and the financial statements of the Company and its subsidiaries for the year ended 31 March 1993.

Principal activities
The principal activities of the Group are Retailing and Financial activities. Financial activities comprise financial services, treasury and insurance. Financial services include Chargecard, Budgetcard, personal loans and the management of unit trusts.

Review of activities and future performance
A review of the Group's activities and of the future development of the Group is contained in the Chairman's statement on pages 2 to 5.

Profit and dividends
The profit for the financial year, after taxation and minority interests, amounts to £495.5m The directors recommend that this be dealt with as follows:

Dividends	£m
Preference shares	0·1
Ordinary shares	
Interim paid, 2·2p per share	
(last year 2·1p)	60·7
Final dividend proposed, 5·9p per share	
(last year 5·0p)	162·8
Total ordinary dividends, 8·1p per share	
(last year 7·1p)	223·5
Undistributed surplus	**271·9**

The proposed final dividend will be paid on 30 July 1993 to shareholders whose names are on the Register of Members at the close of business on 4 June 1993.

Ordinary share capital
During the year ended 31 March 1993, 16,993,288 ordinary shares in the Company were issued as follows:
 a 4,489,391 to the Trustees of the United Kingdom Employees' Profit Sharing Schemes at 329p each, in respect of the allocation from the profits of the year ended 31 March 1992.
 b 384,375 under the terms of the 1977 United Kingdom Senior Staff Share Option Scheme at prices between 137p and 232.333p each.
 c 1,851,837 under the terms of the 1984 United Kingdom Senior Staff Share Option Scheme at prices between 137p and 232.333p each.
 d 1,842,154 under the terms of the 1987 United Kingdom Senior Staff Share Option Scheme at prices between 175p and 202p.

e 5,294,193 under the terms of the United Kingdom Employees' Savings-Related Share Option Scheme at prices between 103p and 257p.

f 3,131,338 issued under the scrip dividend scheme, 2,093,680 in respect of the final dividend for 1991/92 and 1,037,658 in respect of the interim dividend for 1992/93.

Substantial shareholdings
At 12 May 1993 Prudential Corporation p.l.c. and its subsidiaries held 172,885,378 ordinary shares which represented 6.3% of the issued ordinary share capital of the Company. The Company has not received notification that any other person holds more than 3.0% of the issued ordinary share capital.

United Kingdom employees' profit sharing schemes
The amount of profit which will be allocated this year, in the form of ordinary shares in the Company, has been fixed at £18.1m (last year £16.2m), representing 4.8% of the earnings of 42,890 eligible employees.

Fixed assets
Changes in tangible fixed assets during the year are set out in note 16 on pages 43 and 44.

Directors and their interests
The present directors are listed on pages 8 and 9.

Mr R Aldridge, Mr J R Benfield and Mr J T Rowe were appointed directors on 1 January 1993.

Mr J A Lusher retired as a director on 31 December 1992 and Mr A K P Smith resigned as a director on 31 March 1993.

Sir Ralph Robins was appointed as a non-executive director on 1 September 1992.

Dr D V Atterton CBE retired as a non-executive director on 31 July 1992.

In accordance with Article 87 of the Company's Articles of Association, Mr R W C Colvill, Mr P G McCracken, Mr P L Salsbury, Mr A Z Stone and The Rt Hon The Baroness Young retire by rotation and, being eligible, offer themselves for re-election.

In accordance with Article 93 of the Company's Articles of Association, Mr R Aldridge, Mr J R Benfield, Sir Ralph Robins and Mr J T Rowe, retire by rotation and, being eligible, offer themselves for re-election.

Sir Ralph Robins and Baroness Young have service contracts with the Company which have 26 and 16 months to run respectively. None of the other directors to be proposed for re-election at the Annual General Meeting has a contract of more than 12 months' duration with the Company.

The beneficial interests of the directors and their families in the shares of the Company and its subsidiaries, together with their interests as trustees of both charitable and other trusts, are shown in note 33 on page 52.

Directors' interests in contracts or arrangements with the Company during the year are shown in note 32 on page 51.

The Company maintains liability insurance covering the directors and officers of the Company and its subsidiaries.

Brief biographical details of the non-executive directors are provided on pages 8 and 9.

Employee involvement
We have maintained our commitment to employee involvement throughout the business.

Staff are kept well informed of the performance and objectives of the Group through established methods of personal briefings and regular meetings. These are supplemented by our staff publications, *St Michael News* and *M&S World* and video presentations.

'Focus groups' in stores and warehouses allow management to meet with elected staff representations. These groups provide opportunities for staff to contribute to the everyday running of their workplace.

Directors and executives regularly visit stores and discuss with members of staff matters of current interest and concern to the business. Staff representatives attend the Annual General Meeting and all members of staff have the Group results explained in *St Michael News*.

We have long-established Employees' Profit Sharing and Savings-Related Share Option Schemes, memberships of which are service related.

Equal opportunities
The Group does not discriminate against anyone on any grounds. The sole criterion for selection or promotion is the suitability of any applicant for the job. Training and development is provided and available to all levels and categories of staff. The highest positions in the Company are open to all and many supervision and management vacancies are filled by internal transfer and promotion.

Disabled employees
We have continued our policy of giving disabled people full and fair consideration for all job vacancies for which they offer themselves as suitable applicants, having regard to their particular aptitudes and abilities. Training and career development opportunities are available to all employees and if necessary we endeavour to retrain any member of staff who develops a disability during employment with us.

Charitable and political contributions
During the year, we spent £5.8m in the UK in support of the community. Within this, direct donations to charitable organisations amounted to £3,837,000. A political contribution of £10,000 was made to the Conservative Party.

Annual General Meeting Special business resolutions
Explanations of the resolutions are set out below.

Resolution 13
The Companies Act 1985 prevents directors from allotting unissued shares without the authority of shareholders in general meeting. In certain circumstances, this could be unduly restrictive.

The Company's Articles empower your directors to allot unissued shares but the power is subject to annual renewal. Renewal of the power is sought for the period specified in the resolution, subject to the limitations that your directors may only allot:

(i) Shares, in total, equal to the nominal value of the *unissued* share capital of the Company, "the Section 80 Amount".

(ii) Shares for cash up to an amount equal to 5% of the nominal value of the *issued* share capital of the Company as at 31 March 1993, "the Section 89 Amount".

Shareholders' consent to each allotment of shares for cash made otherwise than to existing shareholders in proportion to their existing shareholdings is not required if shareholders approve this resolution.

Resolution 14
The Company's Articles empower the directors to offer ordinary shareholders the right to elect to receive an allotment of additional ordinary shares in lieu of any dividend proposed to be paid or declared at any Annual General Meeting or at any time prior to the next following Annual General Meeting.

The exercise of the power must receive the prior approval of the shareholders in general meeting. That approval is, therefore, sought for the period specified in the resolution.

Income and Corporation Taxes Act 1988
The close company provisions of this Act do not apply to the Company.

Auditors
A resolution proposing the reappointment of Coopers & Lybrand as auditors to the Company will be put to the Annual General Meeting.

By order of the Board
Sir Richard Greenbury, Chairman
London 17 May 1993

Consolidated profit and loss account
For the year ended 31 March 1993

	Notes	1993 £m	1993 £m	1992 [restated] £m	1992 [restated] £m
Turnover					
Continuing operations		5,925·2		5,728·0	
Discontinued operations		25·6		99·5	
	3, 4		5,950·8		5,827·5
Cost of sales	4		3,879·6		3,857·3
Gross profit			2,071·2		1,970·2
Other expenses	4		1,334·5		1,292·5
Operating profit					
Continuing operations		739·9		681·7	
Discontinued operations		(3·2)		(4·0)	
	4		736·7		677·7
Discontinued operations provision used			3·2		1·5
			739·7		679·2
UK profit sharing	13c		18·1		16·2
Loss of sale of fixed assets in continuing operations	5		7·8		8·2
UK head office restructure	6a		—		16·9
Provision for discontinued Canadian operations	6b				
Provision set up		—		59·8	
Cost incurred		43·6		2·3	
Provision used		(43·6)		(2·3)	
			—		59·8
Profit before interest and taxation		714·0			578·1
Net interest receivable	7		22·5		10·8
Profit on ordinary activities before taxation			736·5		588·9
Tax on ordinary activities	8		239·5		218·3
Profit on ordinary activities before taxation			497·0		370·6
Minority interests			1·5		2·6
Profit for the financial year	9		495·5		368·0
Dividends	10		223·6		194·5
Undistributed surplus	25		271·9		173·5
Earnings per share	11		18·0p		13·5p

Balance sheets

At 31 March 1993

	Notes	The Group 1993 £m	1992 restated £m	The Company 1993 £m	1992 restated £m
Fixed assets					
Tangible assets:					
Land and buildings		2,453·4	2,359·0	2,229·2	2,180·2
Fixtures, fittings and equipment		417·1	385·6	317·9	309·8
Assets in the course of construction		38·1	32·1	25·0	18·1
	16	2,908·6	2,776·7	2,572·1	2,508·1
Investments	17	19·4	4·7	554·4	447·0
		2,928·0	2,781·4	3,126·5	2,955·1
Current assets					
Stocks		344·2	338·3	231·8	224·6
Debtors – receivable within one year	18	406·1	358·0	704·4	745·6
– receivable after more than one year	18	323·4	290·2	56·5	57·2
Investments	19	53·9	50·6	22·9	13·4
Cash at bank and in hand	20	634·1	487·7	47·7	43·0
		1,761·7	1,524·8	1,063·3	1,083·8
Current liabilities					
Creditors: amounts falling due within one year	21	1,230·7	1,168·8	733·0	851·3
Net current assets		531·0	356·0	330·3	232·5
Total assets less current liabilities		3,459·0	3,137·4	3,456·8	3,187·6
Creditors: amounts falling due after more than one year	22	446·4	401·5	140·0	140·0
Provisions for liabilities and charges	23	45·7	75·8	35·8	36·4
Net assets		2,966·9	2,660·1	3,281·0	3,011·2
Capital and reserves					
Called up share capital	24	690·6	686·4	690·6	686·4
Share premium account	25	129·7	103·0	129·7	103·0
Revaluation reserve	25	448·9	454·8	464·1	466·0
Profit and loss account	25	1,680·7	1,402·8	1,996·6	1,755·8
Shareholders' funds	25	2,949·9	2,647·0	3,281·0	3,011·2
Minority interests		17·0	13·1	–	–
Total capital employed		2,966·9	2,660·1	3,281·0	3,011·2

Approved by the Board
17 May 1993

Sir Richard Greenbury, Chairman
J K Oates, Managing Director

Consolidated cash flow statement
For the year ended 31 March 1993

	Notes	1993 £m	1992 restated £m
Operating activities			
Net cash received from customers		**5,893·3**	5,775·3
Cash payments to suppliers		**(3,878·7)**	(3,868·0)
Cash paid to and on behalf of employees		**(711·2)**	(709·0)
Other cash payments		**(524·6)**	(476·8)
Net cash inflow from operating activities	26	**778·8**	721·5
Expenditure against exceptional provisions	29	**(15·7)**	(33·3)
Returns on investments and servicing of finance			
Interest received		**51·3**	46·4
Interest paid		**(33·7)**	(31·1)
Dividends paid	29	**(188·3)**	(175·8)
Net cash outflow from returns on investments and servicing of finance		**(170·7)**	(160·5)
Taxation			
UK corporation tax paid		**(201·4)**	(205·5)
Overseas tax paid		**(14·1)**	(10·7)
Tax paid		**(215·5)**	(216·2)
Investing activities			
Purchase of tangible fixed assets		**(254·9)**	(291·9)
Sale of tangible fixed assets		**17·3**	10·2
Purchase of fixed asset investments		**(27·9)**	(4·7)
Sale of fixed asset investments		**13·2**	–
Sale of subsidiary	29	**4·3**	–
Net cash outflow from investing activities		**(248·0)**	(286·4)
Net cash inflow before financing and treasury activities		**128·9**	25·1
Financing and treasury activities			
Shares issued under employees' share schemes		**30·9**	40·0
Other borrowing		**115·2**	10·9
Repayment of amounts borrowed		**(150·0)**	–
(Purchase)/redemption of non-cash equivalent deposits and short term investments	27	**(139·9)**	(119·5)
Net cash outflow from financing and treasury activities		**(143·8)**	(68·6)
Decrease in cash and cash equivalents	27	**(14·9)**	(43·5)
Decrease in net borrowings	28	**135·9**	65·7

Consolidated statement of total recognised gains and losses
For the year ended 31 March 1993

	Notes	1993 £m	1992 restated £m
Profit for the financial year after taxation and minority interests		**495·5**	368·0
Exchange differences on foreign currency translation	25	**(10·1)**	3·6
Total recognised gains and losses relating to the year		**485·4**	371·6
Prior year adjustment	15	**(23·2)**	–
Total recognised gains and losses recognised since the last annual report		**462·2**	371·6

Reconciliation of movements in shareholders' funds

For the year ended 31 March 1993	Notes	1993 £m	1992 £m
Profit for the financial year after taxation and minority interests		**495·5**	368·0
Dividends	10	**223·6**	194·5
		271·9	173·5
Other recognised gains and losses relating to the year (see statement above)		**(10·1)**	3·6
New share capital subscribed	24	**30·9**	40·0
Goodwill credited to the profit and loss account in respect of provision for disposal of business	23, 25	**–**	16·0
Amounts added back to profit and loss account reserve in respect of scrip dividend	25	**10·2**	9·7
Net additions to shareholders' funds		**302·9**	242·8
Shareholders' funds at 1 April (originally £2,427·4m for 1992 before deducting prior year adjustment of £23·2m – see note 15)	25	**2,647·0**	2,404·2
Shareholders' funds at 31 March	25	**2,949·9**	2,647·0

Accounting policies

The financial statements have been prepared in accordance with applicable accounting standards in the United Kingdom, including Financial Reporting Standard 3 'Reporting Financial Performance'. Following the Urgent Issues Task Force pronouncement on post retirement benefits other than pensions, a liability for health insurance of certain past employees has been recognised as a prior year adjustment (see note 15). A summary of the more important group accounting policies, which have been applied consistently, is given below.

Basis of accounting
The financial statements are drawn up on the historical cost basis of accounting, modified to include the valuation of certain United Kingdom properties at 31 March 1988.

Basis of consolidation
The Group financial statements incorporate the financial statements of Marks and Spencer p.l.c. and all its subsidiaries for the year ended 31 March 1993.

Goodwill
Goodwill arising on consolidation is written off to reserves on acquisition. Goodwill attributable to businesses disposed of is written back to reserves brought forward, and charged through the profit and loss account.

Deferred taxation
Deferred taxation is accounted for at anticipated tax rates on differences arising from the inclusion of items of income and expenditure in taxation computations in periods different from those in which they are included in the financial statements. A deferred tax asset or provision is established to the extent that it is likely that an asset or liability will crystallise in the future.

Fixed assets
a) **Capitalised interest**
In arriving at the cost of land and buildings, interest is not capitalised.

b) **Depreciation**
Depreciation is provided to write off the cost or valuation of tangible fixed assets by equal annual instalments at the following rates:
Freehold and leasehold land and buildings over 50 years – 1% or nil (see i below),
Leasehold land and buildings under 50 years – over the remaining period of the lease,
Fixtures, fittings and equipment – $6\frac{1}{3}\%$ to $33\frac{1}{3}\%$ according to the estimated life of the asset.

(i) Given that the lives of the Group's freehold and long leasehold properties are so long and that they are maintained to such a high standard, it is the opinion of the directors, that in most instances the residual values would be sufficiently high to make any depreciation charge immaterial. The directors have based their estimates of residual values on prices prevailing at the time of acquisition or revaluation. Where residual values are lower than cost or valuation, depreciation is charged to the profit and loss account. Any permanent diminution in value is also charged to the revaluation reserve or the profit and loss account as appropriate.

(ii) Depreciation is charged on all additions to depreciating assets in the year of purchase.

c) **Repairs and renewals**
Expenditure on repairs, renewals and minor items of equipment is written off in the year in which it is incurred.

Certain major items of fixed plant are incorporated within the cost of buildings when purchased. When replaced, these are fully expensed as repairs and renewals in the profit and loss account.

Foreign currencies
The results of overseas subsidiaries have been translated at average exchange rates for sales and profits. The balance sheets of overseas subsidiaries have been translated at year end exchange rates or, where appropriate, at the rate of exchange in a related forward exchange contract. The resulting exchange differences are dealt with through reserves.

Transactions denominated in foreign currencies are translated at the exchange rate at the date of the transaction. Foreign currency assets and liabilities held at year end are translated at year end exchange rates or the exchange rate of a related forward exchange contract where appropriate. The resulting exchange gain or loss is dealt with in the profit and loss account.

Pension contributions
The Group operates pension schemes for the benefit of all its United Kingdom employees and for the majority of the staff overseas. The funds of the schemes are administered by Trustees and are separate from the Group. Independent actuaries complete valuations at least every three years. In accordance with their recommendations, annual contributions are paid to the schemes so as to secure the benefits set out in the rules and to allow the periodic augmentation of current pensions. The cost of these and any variations from regular cost arising from actuarial valuations are charged or credited to profits on a systematic basis over the estimated remaining service lives of the employees.

Stocks
Stocks and work in progress are valued at the lower of cost and net realisable value using the retail method.

Trading results
The trading results include transactions at stores up to and including the nearest Saturday to 31 March. All other transactions are included up to 31 March in each year.

Scrip dividends
The amount of dividends taken as shares instead of cash under the scrip dividend scheme are added back to reserves. The nominal value of shares issued under the scheme has been funded out of the share premium account.

Notes to the financial statements

1 Trading period

The results for the year comprise store sales and related costs for the 52 weeks to 27 March 1993. All other activities are for the year to 31 March 1993.

2 Restatement of prior year

Due to the adoption of FRS3 'Reporting Financial Performance', comparative figures have been restated. A statement reconciling the profit before taxation on the pre FRS3 basis to that reported under FRS3 is given below:

	1993	1992
	£m	£m
Profit before taxation – on pre FRS3 basis	**738·4**	623·5
1992 extraordinary charge reclassified as exceptional (see note 6)	–	(29·8)
Restated fixed asset losses on disposal (see note 5)	**(1·9)**	(4·8)
Profit before taxation – on FRS3 basis	**736·5**	588·9

Where 1992 disclosures have been affected they are headed 'restated' with an explanation when appropriate.

3 Segmental information
a Classes of business

Retailing
Turnover represents goods sold to customers outside the Group, less returns and sales taxes.

Financial Activities
Turnover represents the interest and other income attributable to these activities. The turnover attributable to financial activities arises wholly within the United Kingdom and the Channel Islands.

	Retailing		Financial Activities		Total	
	1993	1992	**1993**	1992	**1993**	1992
		restated				restated
	£m	£m	**£m**	£m	**£m**	£m
Turnover						
Sales to third parties	**5,840·9**	5,729·3	**109·9**	98·2	**5,950·8**	5,827·5
Profit						
Operating profit	**706·9**	656·2	**33·0**	23·0	**739·9**	679·2
UK profit sharing					**(18·1)**	(16·2)
Loss on sale of fixed assets					**(7·8)**	(8·2)
Exceptional charges (seen note 6)					–	(76·7)
Net interest receivable					**22·5**	10·8
Profit before taxation					**736·5**	588·9
Net assets						
Operating assets	**2,584·1**	2,480·4	**109·2**	86·9	**2,693·3**	2,567·3
Net allocated assets					**273·6**	92·8
Total net assets					**2,966·9**	2,660·1

Profit before taxation is £702·9m (last year restated £567·7m) for retailing, and £33·6m (last year £21·2m) for financial activities.

3   Segmental information continued
b   **Geographical segments**

	UK & Rep of Ireland		Continental Europe		Rest of the World		Total	
	1993	1992 restated	**1993**	1992 restated	**1993**	1992 restated	**1993**	1992 restated
	£m	£m	**£m**	£m	**£m**	£m	**£m**	£m
Turnover								
Sales to third parties	**5,186·4**	5,077·4	**237·5**	195·0	**526·9**	555·1	**5,950·8**	5,827·5
Profit								
Operating profit	**683·9**	640·1	**27·3**	23·8	**28·7**	15·3	**739·9**	679·2
UK profit sharing							**(18·1)**	(16·2)
Loss on sale of fixed assets							**(7·8)**	(8·2)
Exceptional charges								
(see note 6)							**–**	(76·7)
Net interest receivable							**22·5**	10·8
Profit before taxation							**736·5**	588·9
Net assets								
Operating assets	**2,425·6**	2,309·4	**141·8**	124·6	**125·9**	133·3	**2,693·3**	2,567·3
Net unallocated assets							**273·6**	92·8
Total net assets							**2,966·9**	2,660·1

The value of goods exported directly from the UK, including shipments to overseas subsidiaries, amounted to £232·.2m (last year £206.0m). Shipments to third party customers amounted to £73·3m (last year £62·7m). These third party shipments comprise £57·6m (last year £50·0m) to Continental Europe and £15·7m (last year £12·7m) to the Rest of the World.

The loss on sale of fixed assets is mainly attributable to the UK and Republic of Ireland.

Turnover and operating profits for the Rest of the World comprise the following:

	Turnover		Operating Profit	
	1993	1992 restated	**1993**	1992 restated
	£m	£m	**£m**	£m
USA				
Brooks Brothers (including Japan)	**204·2**	180·7	**12·6**	10·5
Kings Super Markets	**171·7**	161·8	**6·1**	5·1
Corporate expenses	**–**	–	**(0·7)**	(1·1)
	375·9	342·5	**18·0**	14·5
Canada				
Continuing	**84·5**	88·2	**0·1**	(3·0)
Discontinued	**25·6**	99·5	**(3·2)**	(4·0)
Less provision used	**–**	–	**3·2**	1·5
	110·1	187·7	**0·1**	(5·5)
Far East	**40·9**	24·9	**10·6**	6·3
Total for the Rest of the World	**526·9**	555·1	**28·7**	15·3

4 Operating profit

| | 1993 | | | 1992 | | |
	Continuing Operations	Discontinued Operations	Total	Continuing Operations	Discontinued Operations	Total restated
	£m	£m	£m	£m	£m	£m
Turnover	5,925·2	25·6	5,950·8	5,728·0	99·5	5,827·5
Cost of sales	3,862·9	16·7	3,879·6	3,790·9	66·4	3,857·3
Gross profit	2,062·3	8·9	2,071·2	1,937·1	33·1	1,970·2
Staff costs (see note 13b)	681·3	5·0	686·3	677·7	18·0	695·7
Occupancy costs	234·9	4·5	239·4	212·2	12·6	224·8
Repairs, renewals and maintenance to fixed assets	64·0	0·6	64·6	44·9	1·1	46·0
Depreciation	123·1	0·7	123·8	123·5	2·2	125·7
Other costs	219·1	1·3	220·4	197·1	3·2	200·3
Total other expenses	1,322·4	12·1	1.334·5	1,255·4	37·1	1,292·5
1992 provision (see note 6b)	–	3·2	3·2	–	1·5	1·5
Operating profit/(loss)	739·9	–	739·9	681·7	(2·5)	679·2

The directors consider that the nature of the business is such that the analysis of expenses shown above is more informative than that set out in the formats of the Companies Act 1985.

Other expenses include rentals under operating leases, comprising £4·9m for hire of plant and machinery (last year £10·4m) and £79·4m of other rental costs (last year £76·8m).

Included in other costs is the remuneration of the auditors for the audit of £0·9m (last year 0·8m). Also included in other costs is the remuneration of the auditors for the provision of non-audit services to the Company and its UK subsidiary undertakings of £0·5m.

The restatement of 1992 figures is explained on page 26. Discontinued operations, before utilisation of provisions, include the results of Peoples up to the date of disposal in May 1992.

5 Loss on sale of fixed assets

In previous years, any profit or loss on sale of fixed assets has been calculated with reference to the historical cost of the asset, and the corresponding profit or loss has been included within operating profit. In accordance with FRS3, these profits or losses are now calculated with reference to the carrying value of the asset and the corresponding profit or loss disclosed after operating profit. The difference of £1·9m (last year £4·8m) between historical cost and the revalued carrying amount is transferred directly from the revaluation reserve to the profit and loss reserve (see note 25).

6 Exceptional items

a UK head office restructure

The charge of £16·9m last year represents the cost of voluntary redundancies and associated expenses mainly arising from the restructure of the head office.

b Restructure and disposal in Canada

The provision set up last year of £59·8m comprise £30.0m for the costs of downsizing the Marks & Spencer Division and £29·8m for the disposal of the Peoples business, including £16·0m of attributable goodwill. Also included in the provision set up are the operating losses of the discontinued operations since November 1991 when the decision to restructure was made. In accordance with FRS3, the provision for the disposal of

Peoples in last year's accounts has been restated as an exceptional item (see page 26).

The cost incurred against the above provision on the face of the 1993 profit and loss account, includes the £16·0m of goodwill related to the disposal of the Peoples business in May 1992.

7 Interest	1993 £m	1992 £m
Bank and other interest receivable	53·4	40·7
Interest payable (see below)	(30·9)	(29·9)
	22·5	10·8
Interest payable by the Group comprises:		
Bank loans, overdrafts and commercial paper	(23·0)	(15·9)
Debenture loans – repayable within five years	(1·7)	(0·7)
Debenture loans – repayable in more than five years	(1·2)	(2·3)
9·75% Guaranteed notes 1993	(12·4)	(16·2)
8·25% Guaranteed bonds 1996	(8·8)	(10·8)
US$ Promissory note 1998	(21·0)	(21·7)
	(68·1)	(67·6)
Classified as:		
Interest payable	(30·9)	(29·9)
Cost of sales in the trading results of Financial Services	(37·2)	(37·7)
	(68·1)	(67·6)

Total interest receivable amounted to £150·1m (last year £127·7m) of which £96·7m (last year £87·0m) is included in the trading results of Financial Activities and £53·4m (last year £40·7m) as bank and other interest receivable (see above).

Income from listed investments during the year was £4.4m (last year £1.1m).

8 Tax on profit on ordinary activities	1993 £m	1992 £m
The taxation charge comprises:		
Current taxation		
UK corporation tax at 33% (last year 33%)		
Current year	231·3	211·5
Prior years	(9·7)	(7·2)
	221·6	204·3
Double taxation relief	–	(3·8)
	221·6	200·5
Overseas tax	13·5	12·2
	235·1	212·7
Deferred taxation (see note 18)		
Current year	4·4	4·0
Prior years	–	1·6
	4·4	5·6
	239·5	218·3

The tax credit attributable to last year's exceptional items amounted to £5·6m.

9   Profit for the financial year
As permitted by Section 230 of the Companies Act 1985, the profit and loss account of the Company is not presented as part of these financial statements.

The consolidated profit of £495·5m (last year £368·0m) includes £452·3m (last year £308·9m as restated) which is dealt with in the accounts of the Company.

10 Dividends	**1993**	1992
	£m	£m
Preference paid	**0·1**	0·1
Ordinary:		
– Interim of 2·2p per share (last year 2·1p)	**60·7**	57·4
– Proposed final of 5·9p per share (last year 5·0p)	**162·8**	137·0
	223·6	194·5

Under the scrip dividend scheme, £6·9m of the 1991/92 final dividend and £3·3m of the 1992/93 interim dividend were paid by way of shares, and have been added to reserves (see note 25).

11   Earnings per share
The calculation of earnings per ordinary share is based on earnings after tax, minority interests and preference dividends of £495·4m (last year £367·9m as restated), and on 2,748,794,968 ordinary shares (last year 2,728,797,870), being the weighted average number of shares in issue during the year ended 31 March 1993.

The earnings per share figure for last year has been restated onto the basis required by FRS3. The restatement of earnings after tax for the purposes of the calculation comprises the items set out in note 2.

At 31 March 1993, directors, senior employees and retired staff held unexercised options in respect of 15,170,965 ordinary shares (last year 16,797,287). There were options outstanding under the Savings-Related Share Option Scheme in respect of 47,333,902 shares (last year 46,229,679). If all outstanding options had been exercised, the dilution of earnings per share would not have been material.

12   Foreign exchange rates
The principal foreign exchange rates used in the financial statements are as follows (local currency equivalent of £1):

	Sales Average Rate		Profit Average Rate		Balance Sheet Rate	
	1993	1992	**1993**	1992	**1993**	1992
Republic of Ireland	**0·99**	1·09	**0·98**	1·08	**1·00**	1·08
France	**8·75**	9·85	**8·63**	9·83	**8·24**	9·70
Belgium	**53·52**	59·69	**53·46**	59·57	**50·00**	58·95
The Netherlands	**2·93**	3·22	**3·00**	3·26	**2·73**	3·22
Spain	**176·89**	182·07	**176·61**	181·91	**173·10**	180·85
United States	**1·66**	1·74	**1·68**	1·74	**1·51**	1·74
Canada	**2·05**	2·01	**2·03**	2·03	**1·89**	2·07
Hong Kong	**12·64**	13·53	**12·48**	13·50	**11·64**	13·36
Japan	**205·63**	230·80	**205·60**	231·30	**173·00**	231·50

13 Directors and employees

a   The aggregate emoluments of the directors of the Company were:

	1993 £m	1992 £m
Directors' emoluments	4·5	3·9
Pension contributions	0·5	0·4
Annual performance related bonus	0·8	0·7
	5·8	5·0
Pensions paid to former directors	0·1	0·1
Payments made to former directors	0·4	0·6
	6·3	5·7

One director has waived the right to receive emoluments of £1,368 during the year.

The Group introduced an annual bonus scheme for executive directors and divisional directors in 1988. The is based on the achievement of certain profit targets approved by the compensation committee each year. The committee approved a bonus of £0·8m (last year £0·7m) which has been paid *pro rata* to each executive director's basic salary and is included in the total board emoluments of £5·8m (last year £5·0m). A further £0·5m bonus was paid to divisional directors.

Emoluments paid to the Chairman, who was the highest paid director, were:

	1993 £	1992 £
Emoluments	594,620	533,425
Pension contributions	85,500	73,876
Annual performance related bonus	126,506	101,250
	806,626	708,551

The number of directors of the Company performing their duties mainly within the United Kingdom whose emoluments (including bonus but excluding pension contributions) were within the following ranges, are:

Gross Emoluments £	1993	1992	Gross Emoluments £	1993	1992	Gross Emoluments £	1993	1992
720,001 – 725,000	1	–	270,001 – 275,000	1	–	200,001 – 205,000	–	1
630,001 – 635,000	–	1	265,001 – 270,000	1	–	195,001 – 200,000	1	–
545,001 – 550,000	1	–	255,001 – 260,000	1	1	180,001 – 185,000	–	1
490,001 – 495,000	–	1	250,001 – 255,000	1	1	55,001 – 60,000	1	–
460,001 – 465,000	1	–	245,001 – 250,000	–	1	50,001 – 55,000	–	1
400,001 – 405,000	–	1	240,001 – 245,000	–	1	45,001 – 50,000	3	–
325,001 – 330,000	1	–	230,001 – 235,000	2	–	25,001 – 30,000	3	3
295,001 – 300,000	–	2	225,001 – 230,000	2	–	15,001 – 20,000	1	1
280,001 – 285,000	1	–	205,001 – 210,000	–	3	5,001 – 10,000	1	1

13 Directors and employees continued
b   The average weekly number of employees of the Group during the year was:

		1993	1992
UK stores:	Management and supervisory categories	**4,391**	5,136
	Other	**44,008**	46,306
UK head office:	Management and supervisory categories	**1,830**	1,891
	Other	**1,668**	1,857
Financial Services:	Management and supervisory categories	**120**	114
	Other	**516**	446
Overseas		**9,547**	12,144
		62,080	67,894

The decrease in the average weekly number of employees overseas is accounted for by the restructure and disposal of operations in Canada.

If the number of part-time hours worked was converted on the basis of a full working week, the equivalent average number of full-time employees would have been 40,960 (last year 44,460).

The aggregate remuneration and associated costs of Group employees were:

	1993	1992 restated
	£m	£m
Wages and salaries	**563·4**	576·6
Social security costs	**44·1**	43·6
Pension costs (see note 14)	**50·9**	51·9
Staff welfare and other personnel costs	**41·2**	39·5
	699·6	711·6
Classified as:		
Staff costs (see note 4)	**686·3**	695·7
Manufacturing cost of sales	**13·3**	15·9
	699·6	711·6

The 1992 figures above are restated to exclude £0·6m of exceptional non-operating remuneration charged directly to the Canadian provisions under FRS3.

c Profit sharing:
The Trustees of the United Kingdom Employees' Profit Sharing Schemes have been allocated £18·1m (last year £16·2m) with which to subscribe for ordinary shares in the Company. The price of each share is 341p, being the average market price for the three dealing days immediately following the announcement of the results for the year ended 31 March 1993.

d United Kingdom Employees' Savings-Related Share Option Scheme:
Under the terms of the scheme the Board may offer options to purchase ordinary shares in the Company once in each financial year to those employees who enter into an Inland Revenue approved Save As You Earn (SAYE) savings contract. The price at which options may be offered is 80% of the market price for three consecutive dealing days preceding the date of offer. The options may normally be exercised during the period of six months after the completion of the SAYE contract, either five or seven years after entering the scheme.

13   Directors and employees continued
Outstanding options granted under the UK Employees' Savings-Related Share Option Scheme are as follows:

Options granted	Number of shares 1993	1992	Option price
January 1986	432,712	2,155,301	163·0p
January 1987	3,346,979	4,194,162	175·0p
January 1988	3,014,241	5,442,324	182·0p
January 1989	4,600,422	4,988,648	143·0p
January 1990	8,723,353	9,426,123	151·0p
January 1991	7,624,378	8,204,784	182·0p
January 1992	10,457,006	11,039,723	229·0p
January 1993	9,134,811	–	257·0p

14   Pension costs
The Group operates a number of funded defined benefit pension schemes throughout the world.

The assets of the schemes are held in separate trustee administered funds, and amounts are charged to the profit and loss account so as to spread the cost of pensions over employees' service lives with the Group. The pension cost relating to the UK scheme is assessed in accordance with the advice of an independent qualified actuary using the projected unit method, on the basis of triennial valuations.

The total pension cost for the Group was £50·9m (last year £51·9m) of which £5·5m (last year £5·8m) relates to the overseas schemes.

The latest actuarial valuation of the UK scheme was carried out at 1 April 1992. The assumptions which have the most significant effect on the results of the valuation are those relating to the rate of return on investments and the rates of increase in salaries and pensions. It has been assumed that the investment return is 2% higher per annum than future salary increases, with a further 2% differential between salaries and pension increases.

At the date of the latest actuarial valuation, the market value of the assets of the UK scheme was £1,405·8m and the actuarial valuation of these assets represented 106% of the benefits that had accrued to members, after allowing for expected future increases in earnings. The surplus of the actuarial valuation of assets over the benefits accrued to members was £77·8m. This is being spread over six years from 1 April 1992, being the remaining estimated service lives of the existing members, by a reduction in the annual contribution made to the scheme.

The pension costs relating to overseas schemes have been determined in accordance with the advice of independent qualified actuaries.

As shown in note 18 on page 46, the Company has pre-paid a contribution of £49·2m to the UK scheme.

15   Post retirement health benefits
The Company has a commitment to pay all or a proportion of the health insurance premiums for a number of its retired employees and their spouses, the last of whom retired in 1988. There is no commitment in respect of current employees or those who have retired since 1988.

Following a recent pronouncement of the Urgent Issues Task Force, the Company has assessed this liability in accordance with the advice of an independent qualified actuary. The discounted present value at 31 March 1992 of this, assuming premium inflation of 8·5% and an after tax rate of discount of 5·36%, is £34·7m. This has been provided as a prior year adjustment in accordance with the requirements of the U.I.T.F. pronouncement (see note 23).

In addition, a deferred taxation asset has been established at 31 March 1992 of £11·5m, resulting in a total net prior year reserve adjustment for post retirement health benefits of £23·2m.

16   Fixed assets – tangible assets

a

	The Group				The Company			
	Land & buildings	Fixtures, fittings & equipment	Assets in the course of construction	Total	Land & buildings	Fixtures, fittings & equipment	Assets in the course of construction	Total
	£m	£m	£m	£m	£m	£m	£m	£m
Cost or valuation								
At 1 April 1992	2,423·4	790·9	32·1	3,246·4	2,205·5	641·0	18·1	2,864·6
Additions	40·7	132·9	77·2	250·8	18·1	106·1	58·5	182·7
Transfers	62·3	11·3	(73·6)	–	51·6	–	(51·6)	–
Disposals	(28·2)	(106·6)	(0·1)	(134·9)	(19·0)	(85·7)	–	(104·7)
Differences on exchange	28·7	20·6	2·5	51·8	0·8	0·3	–	1·1
At 31 March 1993	2,526·9	849·1	38·1	3,414·1	2,257·0	661·7	25·0	2,943·7
Accumulated depreciation								
At 1 April 1992	64·4	405·3	–	469·7	25·3	331·2	–	356·5
Depreciation for the year	12·0	111·8	–	123·8	4·7	94·3	–	99·0
Disposals	(8·8)	(96·1)	–	(104·9)	(2·4)	(81·9)	–	(84·3)
Differences on exchange	5·9	11·0	–	16·9	0·2	0·2	–	0·4
At 31 March 1993	73·5	432·0	–	505·5	27·8	343·8	–	371·6
Net book value								
At 31 March 1993	2,453·4	417·1	38·1	2,908·6	2,229·2	317·9	25·0	2,572·1
At 31 March 1992	2,359·0	385·6	32·1	2,776·7	2,180·2	309·8	18·1	2,508·1

Analysis of land & buildings at 31 March 1993

	The Group				The Company			
	Freehold	Long Leasehold	Short Leasehold	Total	Freehold	Long Leasehold	Short Leasehold	Total
	£m	£m	£m	£m	£m	£m	£m	£m
At valuation	825·6	466·2	16·2	1,308·0	825·6	466·2	16·2	1,308·0
At cost	637·4	352·8	228·7	1,218·9	501·6	349·6	97·8	949·0
	1,463·0	819·0	244·9	2,526·9	1,327·2	815·8	114·0	2,257·0
Accumulated depreciation	6·6	1·6	65·3	73·5	2·5	1·6	23·7	27·8
Net book value								
At 31 March 1993	1,456·4	817·4	179·6	2,453·4	1,324·7	814·2	90·3	2,229·2
At 31 March 1992	1,402·6	797·3	159·1	2,359·0	1,289·9	794·4	95·9	1,180·2

b   Gerald Eve, chartered surveyors, valued the Company's freehold and leasehold properties in the United Kingdom and the Isle of Man as at 31 March 1982. This valuation was on the basis of open market value for existing use. At 31 March 1988, the directors, after consultation with Gerald Eve, revalued those of the Company's properties which had been valued as at 31 March 1982 (excluding subsequent additions and adjusted for disposals). The directors' valuation was incorporated into the financial statements at 31 March 1988.

16   Fixed assets – tangible assets continued

If the Company's land and buildings had not been valued at 31 March 1982 and 31 March 1988 their net book value would have been:

	1993	1992
	£m	£m
At valuation at 31 March 1975	344·8	347·0
At cost	1,185·0	1,129·6
At 31 March 1993	1,529·8	1,476·6
Accumulated depreciation	70·8	68·9
	1,459·0	1,407·7

The Company also valued its land and buildings in 1955 and in 1964. In the opinion of the directors unreasonable expense would be incurred in obtaining the original costs of the assets valued in those years and in 1975.

c   The Company does not maintain detailed records of cost and depreciation for fixtures, fittings and equipment. The accumulated cost figures represent reasonable estimates of the sums involved.

17   Fixed assets – investments

a

	The Group			The Company			
	Joint venture	Other investments	Total	Shares in subsidiaries	Loans to subsidiaries	Joint venture	Total
	£m	£m	£m	£m	£m	£m	£m
Cost							
At 1 April 1992	4·7	–	4·7	392·3	50·0	4·7	447·0
Additions	0·6	27·3	27·9	106·9	–	0·6	107·5
Disposals	–	(13·2)	(13·2)	–	–	–	–
Repayment of loan	–	–	–	–	(0·1)	–	(0·1)
At 31 March 1993	5·3	14·1	19·4	499·2	49·9	5·3	554·4

The investment in the joint venture represents the Company's 50% holding in Hedge End Park Ltd, a property development company. The joint venture partner is J. Sainsbury plc.

Other investments comprise securities held by a subsidiary.

Additions to shares in subsidiaries represents the refinancing of an existing overseas subsidiary.

The net book value of listed investments included in other investments was as follows:

	£m
Listed on a recognised stock exchange	7·5
Other listed investments	6·6
	14·1
Market value of listed investments at 31 March 1993	14·2

17   Fixed assets – investments continued
b   The Company's principle subsidiaries are set out below. A schedule of interests in all subsidiaries is filed with the Annual Return.

	Principal activity	Country of incorporation and operation	Proportion of shares held by: The Company	A subsidiary
Marks and Spencer International Holdings Limited	Holding Company	Great Britain	100%	–
Marks & Spencer (Nederland) BV	Holding Company	The Netherlands	–	100%
Marks & Spencer US Holdings Inc	Holding Company	United States	100%	–
Marks & Spencer (France) SA	Retailing	France	–	100%
SA Marks and Spencer (Belgium) NV	Retailing	Belgium	–	100%
Marks and Spencer (España) SA	Retailing	Spain	–	67%
Marks and Spencer (Stores) BV	Retailing	The Netherlands	–	100%
Marks and Spencer (Ireland) Limited	Retailing	Republic of Ireland	–	100%
Marks & Spencer Canada Inc	Retailing	Canada	–	100%
D'Allairds Stores Inc	Retailing	Canada	–	100%
Brooks Brothers Inc	Retailing	United States	–	100%
Brooks Brothers, (Japan) Limited	Retailing	Japan	–	51%
Kings Super Markets Inc	Retailing	United States	–	100%
Marks and Spencer (Hong Kong) Limited	Retailing	Hong Kong	–	100%
Marks and Spencer Retail Financial Services Holdings Limited	Holding Company	Great Britain	100%	–
Marks and Spencer Financial Services Limited	Financial Activities	Great Britain	–	100%
Marks and Spencer Unit Trust Management Limited	Financial Activities	Great Britain	–	100%
Marks and Spencer Savings and Investments Limited	Financial Activities	Great Britain	–	100%
St Michael Finance Limited	Financial Activities	Great Britain	100%	–
MS Insurance Limited	Financial Activities	Guernsey	–	100%
Marks and Spencer Finance (Nederland) BV	Finance	The Netherlands	–	100%
Marks & Spencer Finance Inc	Finance	United States	–	100%
Marks and Spencer Finance p.l.c.	Finance	Great Britain	100%	–

All the companies incorporated in Great Britain are registered in England and Wales.

18   Debtors

	The Group 1993 £m	The Group 1992 restated £m	The Company 1993 £m	The Company 1992 restated £m
Amounts receivable within one year:				
Trade debtors and customer balances	**273·5**	242·1	**16·6**	19·6
Amounts owed by Group companies	**–**	–	**588·1**	629·3
Other debtors	**35·3**	34·0	**22·2**	29·4
Prepayments and accrued income	**97·3**	81·9	**77·2**	67·3
	406·1	358·0	**704·4**	745·6
Amounts receivable after more than one year:				
Deferred taxation asset arising on post retirement health benefits	**11·8**	11·5	**11·8**	11·5
Deferred taxation provision arising on short-term timing differences	**(24·0)**	(19·1)	**(21·4)**	(16·8)
	(12·2)	(7·6)	**(9·6)**	(5·3)
Advance corporation tax recoverable on the proposed final dividend	**47·3**	45·7	**47·3**	45·7
	35·1	38·1	**37·7**	40·4
Customer balances	**262·2**	235·2	**–**	–
Other debtors	**26·1**	16·9	**18·8**	16·8
	323·4	290·2	**56·5**	57·2

18   Debtors continued

Other debtors include loans to employees, the majority of which are connected with house purchases. These include an interest-free loan to an officer of the Company, the balance of which amounted to £2,200 at 31 March 1993 (last year £4,080). Transactions with directors are set out in note 32 on page 51.

Prepayments and accrued income include £49·2m in respect of the UK pension scheme for 1993/94 (last year £42·6m in respect of 1992/93).

The movement of £4·6m in the Group's net deferred taxation balances is represented by a charge to the profit and loss account of £4·4m and exchange movements of £0·2m.

19   Current assets – investments

	The Group		The Company	
	1993	1992	**1993**	1992
	£m	£m	**£m**	£m
Investments listed on a recognised stock exchange:				
Government securities	**6·6**	8·7	–	–
Other	**38·3**	5·7	**14·9**	–
Certificates of tax deposit	**8·0**	10·9	**8·0**	10·9
Securities	–	19·6	–	–
Other	**1·0**	5·7	–	2·5
	53·9	50·6	**22·9**	13·4

The market value of the Group's government securities is £7·2m (last year £9·0m) and the market value of other listed investments is £39·5m (last year £5·8m).

20   Cash at bank and in hand

Cash at bank includes commerical paper and short-term deposits with banks and other financial institutions.

21   Creditors: amounts falling due within one year

	The Group		The Company	
	1993	1992	**1993**	1992
	£m	£m	**£m**	£m
9·75% Guaranteed notes 1993	–	150·0	–	–
Bank loans, overdrafts and commercial paper	**388·6**	250·8	**6·6**	16·7
Trade creditors	**153·9**	140·9	**139·0**	119·9
Bills of exchange payable	–	3·7	–	3·7
Amounts owed to Group companies	–	–	**2·9**	169·4
Taxation	**249·9**	227·7	**233·9**	216·1
Social security and other taxes	**22·3**	27·2	**14·1**	19·9
Other creditors	**87·0**	83·4	**56·8**	61·3
Accruals and deferred income	**166·2**	148·1	**116·9**	107·3
Proposed final dividend	**162·8**	137·0	**162·8**	137·0
	1,230·7	1,168·8	**733·0**	851·3

22 Creditors: amounts falling due after more than one year

	The Group 1993 £m	The Group 1992 £m	The Company 1993 £m	The Company 1992 £m
Repayable between two and five years:				
Debenture loan – secured				
6 1/2% – 1989/1994	10·0	10·0	10·0	10·0
8·25% Guaranteed bonds 1996	100·0	100·0	–	–
Amounts owed to Group companies	–	–	100·0	100·0
Other creditors	0·7	2·7	–	–
Repayable in five years or more:				
Debenture loans – secured				
7 1/4% – 1993/1998	15·0	15·0	15·0	15·0
7 3/4% – 1995/2000	15·0	15·0	15·0	15·0
US$ Promissory note 1998	298·9	258·8	–	–
Other creditors	6·8	–	–	–
	446·4	401·5	140·0	140·0

Debenture loans comprise first mortgage debenture stocks which are secured on certain freehold and leasehold properties of the Company. The Company is entitled to redeem the whole or any part of each stock at par, at any time between the two dates shown above.

23 Provisions for liabilities and charges

	The Group £m	The Company £m
At 31 March 1992	41·1	1·7
Prior year adjustment (see note 15)	34·7	34·7
At 1 April 1992	75·8	36·4
Additions for year	0·2	0·2
Utilised during the year	(31·8)	(0·8)
Exchange difference	1·5	–
At 31 March 1993	45·7	35·8

The provision utilised during the year mainly comprises expenditure related to discontinued Canadian operations.

The provisions at 31 March 1993 comprise £34·9m for post retirement health benefits and the remaining amounts for the discontinued Canadian operations.

24 Called up share capital

	The Company 1993 £m	The Company 1992 £m
Authorised:		
3,200,000,000 ordinary shares of 25p each	800·0	800·0
350,000 7·0% cumulative preference shares of £1 each	0·4	0·4
1,000,000 4·9% cumulative preference shares of £1 each	1·0	1·0
	801·4	801·4
Allotted, called up and fully paid:		
2,757,008,095 ordinary shares of 25p each (last year 2,740,014,807)	689·2	685·0
350,000 7·0% cumulative preference shares of £1 each	0·4	0·4
1,000,000 4·9% cumulative preference shares of £1 each	1·0	1·0
	690·6	686·4

24   Called up share capital continued

13,861,950 ordinary shares having a nominal value of £3·4m were allotted during the year under the terms of the Company's share schemes which are described in notes 13 and 31. The aggregate consideration received was £30·9m. Contingent rights to the allotment of shares are also described in notes 13 and 31. In addition, 3,131,338 shares with a nominal value of £0·8m were allotted to shareholders making an election for scrip dividends. The nominal value of £0·8m in respect of scrip dividends was funded out of the share premium account.

25   Shareholders' funds

	The Group		The Company	
	1993	1992 restated	1993	1992 restated
	£m	£m	£m	£m
Called up share capital (see note 24)	690·6	686·4	690·6	686·4
Share premium account:				
At 1 April	103·0	69·3	103·0	69·3
Shares issued relating to scrip dividend	(0·8)	(0·9)	(0·8)	(0·9)
Movement during the year	27·5	34·6	27·5	34·6
At 31 March	129·7	103·0	129·7	103·0
Revaluation reserve:				
At 1 April	454·8	459·7	466·0	470·8
Realised during the year (see note 5)	(1·9)	(4·8)	(1·9)	(4·8)
Exchange movement	(4·0)	(0·1)	–	–
At 31 March	448·9	454·8	464·1	466·0
Profit and loss account:				
At 1 April	1,402·8	1,218·3	1,755·8	1,650·0
Amounts written back in respect of goodwill	–	16·0	–	–
Amounts added back in respect of scrip dividends (see note 10)	10·2	9·7	10·2	9·7
Realised revaluation reserve (see note 5)	1·9	4·8	1·9	4·8
Undistributed surplus for the year	271·9	173·5	228·7	114·4
Exchange movement	(6·1)	3·7	–	0·1
	1,680·7	1,426·0	1,996·6	1,799·0
Prior year adjustment (see note 15)	–	(23·2)	–	(23·2)
At 31 March	1,680·7	1,402·8	1,996·6	1,755·8
Shareholders' funds	2,949·9	2,647·0	3,281·0	3,011·2

Cumulative goodwill of £462·9m (last year £462·9m) arising on the acquisition of US, Canadian and Spanish subsidiaries has been written off against the profit and loss account in the years of acquisition.

26 Cash Flow Statement: Reconciliation of operating profit to net cash inflow from operating activities

	1993 £m	1992 £m
Operating profit	**739·9**	679·2
Less profit sharing	**(18·1)**	(16·2)
	721·8	663·0
Depreciation	**123·8**	125.7
(Increase)/Decrease in stocks	**(26·7)**	12·8
(Increase)/in debtors	**(83·6)**	(28·2)
Increase/(Decrease) in creditors	**43·5**	(51·8)
Net cash inflow from operating activities	**778·8**	721·5

The working capital movements above exclude the amounts related to the disposal of the subsidiary (see note 29).

27 Cash Flow Statement: Analysis of the balances of cash and cash equivalents in the balance sheet

	1993 £m	1992 £m	1991 £m	Change in 1993 £m	Change in 1992 £m
Investments	**4·7**	11·7	1·2	**(7·0)**	10·5
Cash at bank and in hand	**346·5**	329·8	243·2	**16·7**	86·6
Bank loans, overdrafts and commercial paper	**(262·5)**	(239·2)	(100·0)	**(23·3)**	(139·2)
	88·7	102·3	144·4	**(13·6)**	(42·1)

The decrease in cash and cash equivalents of £13·6m (last year £42·1m), comprises £14·9m (last year £43·5m) analysed in the cash flow statement, offset by a £1·3m (last year £1·4m) gain on foreign exchange rate changes.

Within the balance sheet the above classifications include certain items which, in accordance with the requirements of FRS1, are not shown as cash or cash equivalents for the purposes of the cash flow statement. These include short term deposits and investments with original maturities of more than 90 days and less than one year. These account for the £139·9m net purchase of non-cash equivalent deposits and short term investments in the 1993 cash flow statement.

28 Cash Flow Statement: Analysis of net Group borrowings

	1993 £m	1992 £m	1991 £m	Change in 1993 £m	Change in 1992 £m
Creditors: Amounts falling due after more than one year	**446·4**	401·5	549·6	**44·9**	(148·1)
Less: Amounts not classified in borrowings	**(7·5)**	(2·7)	(0·8)	**(4·8)**	(1·9)
9·75% Guaranteed notes due within one year	**–**	150·0	–	**(150·0)**	150·0
Bank loans, overdrafts and commercial paper	**388·6**	250·8	100·0	**137·8**	150·8
Cash at bank and in hand	**(634·1)**	(487·7)	(293·0)	**(146·4)**	(194·7)
Current asset investments	**(53·9)**	(50·6)	(28·8)	**(3·3)**	(21·8)
Fixed asset investments	**(14·1)**	–	–	**(14·1)**	–
Net Group borrowings	**125·4**	261·3	327·0	**(135·9)**	(65·7)

29   Cash Flow Statement: Sundry notes

On 23 May 1992 the Group disposed of Peoples Department Stores Inc. to Wise Stores Inc. The net assets disposed of comprised fixed assets of £5·0m, stock of £20·7m, debtors of £0·6m less creditors of £5·6m. The consideration received comprised cash of £4·3m and a loan note of £9·4m.

Dividends paid include £0·6m (last year £0·5m) paid to minority shareholders in subsidiaries.

The 1992 figure of £33·3m for exceptional items (previously published as £33·8m) has been restated to exclude the cash flows related to the trading of the discontinued Canadian operations. Following the adoption of FRS3, these amounts are now allocated to the relevant operating cash flow headings.

30 Commitments and contingent liabilities	The Group		The Company	
	1993	1992	**1993**	1992
	£m	£m	**£m**	£m
a Commitments in respect of properties in the course of development	**212·3**	127·2	**187·2**	82·1
b Capital expenditure authorised by the directors but not yet contracted	**297·3**	525·2	**252·7**	384·5
c Deferred taxation not provided on the excess of capital allowances over depreciation on tangible assets	**157·0**	142·6	**148·6**	136·5
d Guarantees by the Company in respect of the Eurobond and Promissory note issued by subsidiaries	–	–	**398·9**	508·8
e Guarantees by the Company of the Commercial Paper issued by St Michael Finance Limited	–	–	**89·9**	55·6
f Guarantees in relation to certain property lease disposals	**9·0**	–	**9·0**	–
g Guarantees by the Company of the liabilities of Marks and Spencer (Nederland) BV, Marks and Spencer (Stores) BV, Marks and Spencer Ireland) Limited	–	–	**11·8**	21·4

Marks and Spencer (Ireland) Limited has availed itself of the exemption provided for in s17 of the Companies (Amendment) Act 1986 (Ireland) in respect of the documents required to be annexed to its annual return.

h In the opinion of the directors, the revalued properties will be retained for use in the business and the likelihood of any taxation liability arising is remote. Accordingly the potential deferred taxation in respect of these properties has not been quantified.

i Other material contracts

In the event of a change in the trading arrangements with certain warehouse operators, the Company has a commitment to purchase, at market value, fixed assets which are currently owned and operated by them on the Company's behalf.

j Commitments under operating leases

At 31 March 1993 annual commitments under operating leases were as follows:

30 Commitments and contingent liabilities continued

	The Group Land & buildings £m	Other £m	The Company Land & buildings £m	Other £m
Expiring within one year	12·3	1·2	–	0·7
Expiring in the second to fifth years inclusive	21·4	2·6	1·1	2·3
Expiring in five years or more	57·1	–	35·8	–
	90·8	3·8	36·9	3·0

31 United Kingdom Senior Staff Share Option Schemes

Under the terms of the 1984 and 1987 schemes, following the announcement of the Company's results, the Board may offer options to purchase ordinary shares in the Company to executive directors and senior employees at the higher of the nominal value of the shares and the average market price for three consecutive dealing days preceding the date of the offer. The 1977 scheme has now expired and no further options may be granted under this scheme. Although options may be granted under both the 1984 and 1987 schemes, the maximum option value that can be exercised under each scheme is limited to four times earnings. Outstanding options offered under all senior schemes are as follows:

Options offered	Number of shares 1993	1992	Option price	Option dates
(1977 Scheme)				
May 1986	**99,186**	248,199	211·000p	May 1989 – May 1993
May 1987	**318,323**	483,825	232·333p	May 1990 – May 1994
(1984 Scheme)				
October 1984	**769,149**	769,149	115·667p	Oct 1987 – Oct 1994
May 1985	**199,497**	223,584	137·000p	May 1988 – May 1995
May 1986	**77,028**	95,037	211·000p	May 1989 – May 1996
May 1987	**333,051**	495,906	232·333p	May 1990 – May 1997
October 1987	**400,986**	481,484	202·000p	Oct 1990 – Oct 1997
May 1988	**1,055,996**	1,305,400	176·000p	May 1991 – May 1998
October 1988	**29,424**	29,424	158·000p	Oct 1991 – Oct 1998
May 1989	**1,488,360**	2,747,147	175·000p	May 1992 – May 1999
May 1990	**2,976,245**	2,982,917	206·000p	May 1993 – May 2000
May 1991	**3,640,246**	3,640,246	254·000p	May 1994 – May 2001
May 1992	**3,394,066**	–	329·000p	May 1995 – May 2002
(1987 Scheme)				
October 1987	**567,984**	645,755	202·000p	Oct 1990 – Oct 1994
May 1988	**2,433,110**	3,064,513	176·000p	May 1991 – May 1995
May 1989	**1,854,170**	2,996,692	175·000p	May 1992 – May 1996
October 1989	**15,038**	61,038	188·000p	Oct 1992 – Oct 1996
May 1990	**3,704,535**	3,720,915	206·000p	May 1993 – May 1997
May 1991	**2,923,254**	2,942,151	254·000p	May 1994 – May 1998
May 1992	**1,925,596**	–	329·000p	May 1995 – May 1999

No options were offered in October 1990, 1991 or 1992.

32 Transactions with directors

Interest-free loans were made under the employees' loan scheme, by the Company to the following, prior to their appointment as directors:

	Dates of loans	At 31 March 1993 £	At 31 March 1992 or date of appointment £
Mr P P D Smith	1987	–	19,880
Mr R Aldridge	1986-1989	–	29,712
Mr J T Rowe	1988	–	15,600

The balances at 31 March 1992 or date of appointment were the highest balances in the year.

33 Directors' interests in shares and debentures

The beneficial interests of the directors and their families in the shares of the Company and its subsidiaries, together with their interests as trustees of both charitable and other trusts, are shown below. These include options granted under the Savings-Related Share Option and Senior Staff Share Option Schemes, and shares held under the Delayed Profit Sharing Scheme. Further information regarding employee share options is given in notes 13d and 31 on pages 41 and 51.

Ordinary shares in the Company – beneficial and family interests

	Shares		Options			
	At 1 April 1992 or date of appointment	At 31 March 1993	At 1 April 1992 or date of appointment	Granted in year	Exercised/ lapsed in year	At 31 March 1993
Sir Richard Greenbury	21,062	26,094	372,079	97,087	262,856	206,310
C V Silver	47,106	52,256	295,889	54,379	182,856	167,412
J K Oates	17,739	21,119	863,470	44,094	10,000	897,564
R Aldridge	16,928	16,298	405,125	–	81,710	323,415
J R Benfield	17,678	11,687	303,409	–	94,680	208,729
N L Colne	66,479	70,542	665,993	58,754	23,696	701,051
R W C Colvill	13,230	15,676	411,003	30,315	128,736	312,582
C Littmoden	19,214	18,261	264,995	19,419	95,611	188,803
P G McCracken	8,922	11,256	211,356	18,645	74,476	155,525
J T Rowe	11,045	11,106	186,946	–	63,998	122,948
S J Sacher	399,194	343,640	464,570	36,928	–	501,498
P L Salsbury	22,069	24,712	300,545	21,360	126,092	195,813
The Hon David Sieff	296,402	299,206	496,467	58,903	–	555,370
A K P Smith	186,113	390,520	694,214	47,469	641,544	100,139
P P D Smith	7,393	7,556	297,824	22,858	310,000	10,682
A Z Stone	11,232	13,546	299,854	31,068	144,913	186,009
D G Trangmar	38,045	41,391	103,981	15,534	–	119,515
Sir Martin Jacomb	6,665	6,665	–	–	–	–
D G Lanigan	3,103	3,527	9,456	–	–	9,456*
Sir Ralph Robins	2,000	2,013	–	–	–	–
D R Susman	58,863	60,164	–	–	–	–
The Rt Hon The Baroness Young	3,847	4,201	–	–	–	–

*Non-executive directors are not eligible for the Senior Staff Share Option Schemes. Mr Lanigan's options are held under the Savings-Related Share Option Scheme which is open to all members of staff.

33   Directors' interests in shares and debentures continued
Ordinary shares in the Company – trustee interests

	At 31 March 1993		At 1 April 1992	
	Charitable Trusts Shares	Other Trusts Shares	Charitable Trusts Shares	Other Trusts Shares
S J Sacher	85,000	168,118	205,000	170,118
The Hon David Sieff	12,000	81,636	20,000	87,542
D R Susman	570,100	–	570,100	–

Preference shares and debentures
At 31 March 1993 Mr N L Colne owned 500 4·9% preference shares (last year 500 shares). Mr C Littmoden owned 10 4·9% preference shares and 10 7% preference shares (last year 10 4·9% preference shares and 10 7% preference shares). No other director had an interest in any preference shares or debentures of the Company.

No directors had any interests in any subsidiary at the beginning or end of the year.

Between the end of the financial year and one month prior to the date of the Notice of Meeting, all options granted to Mr A K P Smith lapsed on the date of his resignation as an employee. There have been no other changes in the directors' interests in shares and debentures of, or in options granted by, the Company and its subsidiaries.

Directors' responsibilities and Report of the auditors

Directors' responsibilities for preparing the financial statements

The directors are obliged under company law to prepare financial statements for each financial year and to present them annually to the Company's members in Annual General Meeting.

The financial statements, of which the form and content is prescribed by the Companies Act 1985, must give a true and fair view of the state of affairs of the Company and the Group at the end of the financial year, and of the profit for that period, and they must comply with applicable accounting standards.

The directors are also responsible for the adoption of suitable accounting policies, their consistent use in the financial statements, supported where necessary by reasonable and prudent judgements.

The directors confirm that the above requirements have been complied with in the financial statements.

In addition, the directors are responsible for maintaining adequate accounting records and sufficient internal controls to safeguard the assets of the Group and to prevent and detect fraud or any other irregularities.

Report of the auditors

To the members of Marks and Spencer p.l.c.

We have audited the financial statements on pages 30 to 52.

Respective responsibilities of directors and auditors

As described above the Company's directors are responsible for the preparation of financial statements. It is our responsibility to form an independent opinion, based on our audit, on those statements and to report our opinion to you.

Basis of opinion

We conducted our audit in accordance with Auditing Standards issued by the Auditing Practices Board. An audit includes examination, on a test basis, of evidence relevant to the amounts and disclosures in the financial statements. It also includes an assessment of the significant estimates and judgements made by the directors in the preparation of the financial statements, and of whether the accounting policies are appropriate to the Company's circumstances, consistently applied and adequately disclosed.

We planned and performed our audit so as to obtain all the information and explanations which we considered necessary in order to provide us with sufficient evidence to give reasonable assurance that the financial statements are free from material misstatement, whether caused by fraud or other irregularity or error. In forming our opinion we also evaluated the overall adequacy of the presentation of information in the financial statements.

Opinion

In our opinion the financial statements give a true and fair view of the state of affairs of the Company and the Group at 31 March 1993 and of the profit, total recognised gains and cash flows of the Group for the year then ended and have been properly prepared in accordance with the Companies Act 1985.

Coopers & Lybrand
Chartered Accountants and Registered Auditors
London
17 May 1993

The capital of the Group arises from the following sources:

1 Preference shares

The 1,350,000 preference shares are held by 579 shareholders, who receive dividends in preference to the holders of ordinary shares at rates of 4·9% and 7% per annum, plus related tax credit.

2 Ordinary shares

There are 301,152 holders of ordinary shares who receive dividends at rates declared either by the directors or at the Annual General Meeting. Their shareholdings are analysed as follows:

Size of shareholding	Number of shareholders	Percentage of total number of shareholders	Number of ordinary shares 000s	Percentage of ordinary shares
Over 1,000,000	302		1,595,246	57·9
500,001 – 1,000,000	208		151,087	5·5
200,001 – 500,000	399	0·7	129,336	4·7
100,001 – 200,000	449		65,112	2·3
50,001 – 100,000	875		62,074	2·2
20,001 – 50,000	3,489	1·2	104,943	3·8
10,001 – 20,000	8,828	2·9	122,587	4·5
5,001 – 10,000	22,985	7·6	161,328	5·8
2,001 – 5,000	65,574	21·8	209,127	7·6
1,001 – 2,000	68,352	22·7	100,890	3·7
501 – 1,000	52,989	17·6	40,445	1·5
1 – 500	76,702	25·5	14,833	0·5
	301,152	100·0	2,757,008	100·0

3 Debenture loans

These loan stocks, with a nominal value of £40m, are owned by Prudential Assurance Company Ltd and Prudential Nominees Ltd who are entitled to interest at annual rates ranging from 6·5% to 7·75% under the terms of the debenture trust deed.

4 8.25% Guaranteed bonds 1996

US$150m was raised in 1986 by the issue of a Eurobond at an annual interest rate of 8.25% maturing in 1996. Currency and interest swaps were arranged to provide £100m at floating interest rates below LIBOR.

5   US$ Promissory note 1998
A US$450m ten year Promissory note, bearing interest at LIBOR, was issued by a subsidiary of Marks and Spencer p.l.c. as part of the finance for the acquisition of Brooks Brothers.

6   Bank loans, overdrafts and commercial paper
Bank loans, overdrafts and commercial paper have been obtained to finance certain of the Company's subsidiaries and the overdrafts bear interest at rates varying with local bank rates.

7   9.75% Guaranteed notes 1993 redeemed
£150m was raised in 1988 by the issue of a Eurobond. This was redeemed on maturity in March 1993.

We can apply the ratios we have described to these accounts for the purpose of analysis.

1. **Profitability ratios**	1992	1993

A. Gross profit to net capital employed

$$\frac{\text{Gross profit} \times 100}{\text{Net capital employed}} \qquad \frac{1970 \cdot 2 \times 100}{3137 \cdot 4} = 62 \cdot 8\% \qquad \frac{2071 \cdot 2 \times 100}{3459} = 59 \cdot 9\%$$

B. Net profit to net capital employed

$$\frac{\text{Profit on ordinary activities before tax} \times 100}{\text{Net capital employed}} \qquad \frac{588 \cdot 9 \times 100}{3137 \cdot 4} = 18 \cdot 8\% \qquad \frac{736 \cdot 5 \times 100}{3459} = 21 \cdot 3\%$$

C. Gross profit percentage of sales

$$\frac{\text{Gross profit} \times 100}{\text{Sales}} \qquad \frac{1970 \cdot 2 \times 100}{5827 \cdot 5} = 33 \cdot 8\% \qquad \frac{2071 \cdot 2 \times 100}{5950 \cdot 8} = 34 \cdot 8\%$$

D. Net profit percentage of sales

$$\frac{\text{Net profit} \times 100}{\text{Sales}} \qquad \frac{588 \cdot 9 \times 100}{5827 \cdot 5} = 10 \cdot 1\% \qquad \frac{736 \cdot 5 \times 100}{5950 \cdot 8} = 12 \cdot 4\%$$

2. **Short-term liquidity ratios**

A. Current ratio

Current assets : current liabilities $1524 \cdot 8 : 1168 \cdot 8 = 1 \cdot 3 : 1$ $1761 \cdot 7 : 1230 \cdot 7 = 1 \cdot 4 : 1$

B. Quick ratio

Quick assets : current liabilities $896 \cdot 3 : 1168 \cdot 8 = 0 \cdot 8 : 1$ $1094 \cdot 1 : 1230 \cdot 7 = 0 \cdot 9 : 1$

Quick assets excludes stocks and debtors
receivable after more than one year

3. **Long-term solvency ratio**

Gearing ratio $\dfrac{401 \cdot 5 \times 100}{2647} = 15 \cdot 2\%$ $\dfrac{446 \cdot 4 \times 100}{2949 \cdot 9} = 15 \cdot 1\%$

Long-term debt as a percentage of shareholders'
funds

4. Efficiency ratios   1992   1993

A. Collection period for debts (Age of debtors)

$$\frac{\text{Turnover}}{\text{Trade debtors (Note 18)}}$$ $\frac{5827\cdot5}{242\cdot1} = 24 \text{ times}$ $\frac{5950\cdot8}{273\cdot5} = 22 \text{ times}$

Turnover debtors $\frac{52}{24} = 2\cdot2 \text{ weeks}$ $\frac{52}{22} = 2\cdot4 \text{ weeks}$

B. Payment period for creditors (Age of creditors)

$$\frac{\text{Cost of sales}}{\text{Trade creditors (Note 21)}}$$ $\frac{3857\cdot3}{140\cdot9} = 27 \text{ times}$ $\frac{3879\cdot6}{153\cdot9} = 25 \text{ times}$

Turnover creditors $\frac{52}{27} = 1\cdot9 \text{ weeks}$ $\frac{52}{25} = 2\cdot1 \text{ weeks}$

C. Rate of stock turnover

$$\frac{\text{Cost of sales}}{\text{Year end stock}}$$ $\frac{3857\cdot3}{338\cdot3} = 11 \text{ times}$ $\frac{3879\cdot6}{344\cdot2} = 11 \text{ times}$

Turnover stock $\frac{52}{11} = 4\cdot7 \text{ weeks}$ $\frac{52}{11} = 4\cdot7 \text{ weeks}$

D. Fixed asset turnover

$$\frac{\text{Turnover}}{\text{Fixed assets}}$$ $\frac{5827\cdot5}{2776\cdot7} = 2\cdot1 \text{ times}$ $\frac{5950\cdot8}{2908\cdot6} = 2 \text{ times}$

E. Sales per employee

$$\frac{\text{Turnover}}{\text{Number of Employees (Note 13)}}$$ $\frac{5827\cdot5 \text{ million}}{67894} = £85,832$ $\frac{5950\cdot8 \text{ million}}{62080} = £95,857$

Now you have calculated the ratios, what have they told you about Marks and Spencer? What additional information would be helpful in getting a feel for the company's performance?

Chapter 10

Financial Implications of Personnel Decisions

The main decisions of the Personnel Manager concern human resources but there are others which are important, as for example the purchase of capital equipment or the offering of training services outside the employing organization. Each of these decisions will generate both costs and revenues and it is essential that the Personnel Manager fully appreciates their implications. A more detailed discussion of this important topic appears in Hugo Fair's *Personnel and Profit: The payoff from people* (IPM, 1992).

People are essential to the success of all organizations. They are the major asset of any undertaking but they are also a major cost. It is because of this that organizations are keen to ensure that they are using their people effectively, efficiently and economically. In the private sector a key ratio that is successfully employed is sales per employee (see the analysis of Marks and Spencer's accounts in chapter 9). Do you know what this figure is in your business? You should be aware that if you recruit additional people it will have an immediate impact on the sales per employee ratio. This ratio, like the others we have considered, should never be looked at in isolation. Trends are significant, as are comparisons with other similar businesses. Using the manufacturing account example in chapter 8, and assuming that there are 5,000 employees, we can calculate the sales per employee to be:

$$\frac{\text{Sales}}{\text{Employees}} = \frac{7,600,000}{5,000} = £1,520$$

If you were presented with this figure in isolation your reaction would probably be, 'so what!' In order to be meaningful it has to be compared with something. If sales per employee had been £2,000 for the last four years and it suddenly fell to £1,520 you would want to know why and correct the situation if possible. Recruitment of additional staff would have an impact on the ratio unless you were immediately able to generate proportionally higher sales. For example, an extra 100 staff would make the sales per employee:

$$\frac{7,600,000}{5,100} = £1,490.20$$

This fall of nearly £30 per employee would have to be recovered as quickly as possible. Sales are not as critical in the public sector as they are in the private sector, so the above ratio would not apply. But it might be replaced by such ratios as refuse collected per employee, houses painted per employee or meals served per employee.

This concentration on the activity per employee has led many organizations, and managers within them to believe that the way to save money and operate more effectively is by reducing the number of staff. There is a great emphasis on head-count and the Personnel Manager has to demonstrate the added value provided by staff, particularly his or her own department. It is incumbent on the Personnel Manager to provide information that demonstrates the efficiency of the department, and if this can be achieved through the use of ratios so much the better. One ratio which is commonly used for this purpose is the cost of human resources, which is calculated by dividing the total expenses of the organization into the expenses of each department. If the expenses of an organization are £6,740,000 and of the Personnel, Manufacturing, Sales and Marketing departments £960,000, £3,400,000, £1,230,000 and £1,150,000 respectively, then the ratio for each department becomes:

Personnel $\qquad \dfrac{£\ 960,000}{£6,740,000} \times 100 = 14.2\%$

Manufacturing $\qquad \dfrac{£3,400,000}{£6,740,000} \times 100 = 50.4\%$

Sales $\qquad \dfrac{£1,230,000}{£6,740,000} \times 100 = 18.2\%$

Marketing $\qquad \dfrac{£1,150,000}{£6,740,000} \times 100 = 17.1\%$

This could then be illustrated as in figure 7:

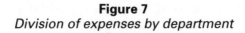

Figure 7
Division of expenses by department

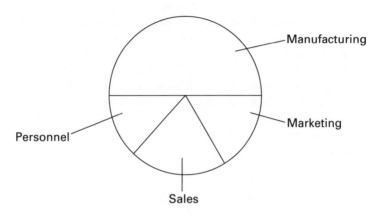

Manufacturing

Marketing

Personnel

Sales

To be able to undertake such an investigation the Personnel Manager would require more information than is provided by the traditional financial accounts, and it is for reasons like this that the cost accounts, to which we will be introduced in the next chapter, were developed.

The capital investment decision has a major impact on the organization; by its nature it uses a large proportion of the available money and may carry over for more than one financial year. If for example the Personnel Manager requires a new training wing costing £4 million it is extremely unlikely that the proposal will be accepted unless the budgeted benefits can be seen to exceed the costs by a satisfactory amount. It is no use talking in general terms about the benefits that will accrue to the organization from such a step. Estimates have to be made of the savings and/or income that will be generated by the scheme and they must be compared with the outlay. The Personnel Manager will then be able to build a case for the proposal and hopefully demonstrate its advantages over competing bids for the available funds for capital outlay. This can employ such tools as pay-back, which demonstrates how quickly the expenditure is recovered, and net present value, which compares the outlay with the estimate of funds to be generated in present value terms. These approaches are discussed in greater detail in chapter 18.

Many organizations are now offering expertise that they previously employed internally to the open market. Training is one such service and it is reasonable that this should be done. Organizations that have been proactive in training and development over the last six years have found that other organizations are prepared to pay well for their expertise. But the Personnel Manager should not embark on such a course of action without fully considering the attendant costs and benefits. There is more than one way of calculating the costs of such a venture. If the full-cost approach is adopted, all costs would have to be recovered plus the required profit. This approach is fully discussed in chapter 12. On the other hand, the concept of contribution may be applied, using the marginal costing approach. Here only those costs directly involved in providing the additional training are considered; anything over and above that makes a contribution to the department's fixed costs. Chapter 14 covers this approach in greater detail.

All personnel decisions have financial implications and personnel managers need detailed financial information. The provision of this information is discussed in the remainder of the book.

Chapter 11

Costing

The information systems that have been dealt with so far have been concerned with financial information for planning and reporting, with some control elements. In chapter 8 manufacturing accounts were discussed, and it was suggested that these lend themselves to calculating the cost per unit produced. Because information of this nature is the basis for exercising control in an organization, it will be investigated more fully.

The accounts that we have dealt with so far are the financial accounts, which give an overview of the position of an organization. Whilst this information can help personnel and other managers, control the finances for which she or he is responsible and in making bids for resources, more detailed information is required if costs are to be controlled and plans monitored. This is provided by the cost accounts, which must be capable of being reconciled with the financial accounts at all times. Costing is the process of analysing the expenditure of an organization into the separate costs for each of the services or products supplied to customers.

The way in which the cost and financial accounts may be reconciled can be shown in the following simple example.

Example 18

Financial Accounts

	£(000)
Earnings	1,432
Expenses	1,141
Profit	291

Cost Accounts

Service	£(000) Cleaning	£(000) Security	£(000) Training	£(000) Transport	£(000) Total
Earnings	680	415	123	214	1,432
Expenses	630	372	9	130	1,141
Profit	50	43	114	84	291

Without the benefit of the cost accounts, the planning team might have been inclined to concentrate on cleaning, which generates the-largest earnings. An examination of the cost accounts, however, clearly shows that training gives the greatest profit and would possibly be an appropriate area to develop. Cost accounts can thus assist the Personnel Manager in making a case for the contribution made by the Personnel Department to the health of the organization as a whole. But, as I have said, it is essential for the cost accounts to be reconciled with the financial accounts. If they are not they are of no value to managers and their preparation is a waste of time.

The purposes of costing can be said to be to:

- enable work in progress and finished goods to be valued for short-term and annual accounts
- provide the basis for tenders, pricing policies and estimates
- maintain control over costs
- provide information to ensure that decisions are made on the correct basis.

The costs of each department consist of three elements of:

- labour
- materials
- overheads.

These three elements are further broken down into direct costs, which are charged directly to the service or product, and indirect costs, which are apportioned to the service or product on some equitable basis, as discussed in chapter 12. The cost accounts and the financial accounts are combined in the following way:

	Direct labour
+	Direct materials
+	Direct expense
=	PRIME COST
+	Factory overhead
=	PRODUCTION COST
+	Selling and distribution overhead
+	Selling and distribution direct expense
+	Administration overhead
=	COST OF SALES taken from EARNINGS
=	**NET PROFIT**

The manager also needs to know whether the costs with which she or he is dealing are fixed—that is they remain constant for any level of activity within prescribed limits—or whether they are variable—they vary directly with changes in the level of activity. An example of a fixed cost might be staff salaries in a department which employed three trainers, each capable of training between 10 and 20 people. Their combined salaries would be £51,000, whether they were training 30 or 60 people a week. However, if they were asked to train 100 people a week the departmental salary bill would become £68,000 because an additional trainer would have to be employed. The fixed cost line on a graph would then appear as in figure 8.

Figure 8
Fixed costs in a training department

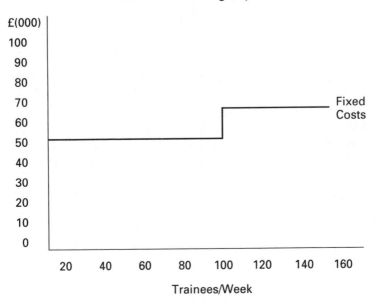

A variable cost would be the cost of the information pack and other materials given to each trainee on the programme. Taking the cost per trainee as £50 the variable cost line could be illustrated as in figure 9.

Figure 9
Variable costs in training department

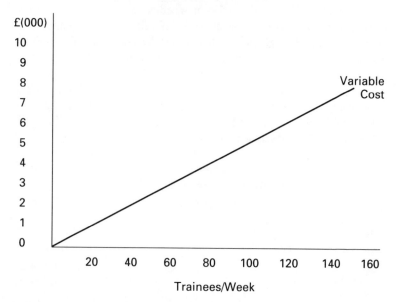

You can see from this that if there were no trainees the cost would be zero, whilst for 100 the cost is £5,000. This is helpful to the Personnel Manager in costing the service provided against the revenues generated by it.

The next three chapters describe various costing methods and their application to the Personnel Manager. They also contain examples of the ways in which they can be calculated and used.

Chapter 12

Absorption Costing

Standard costing is useful in enabling managers to calculate the expected cost of a unit of production or time. Absorption costing, or total costing as it is sometimes called, helps to ensure that organizational costs are fully recovered when a price is quoted for a job or a unit of consultancy. Because little can be done to alter fixed costs in the short term, they are often overlooked when prices are being calculated, with disastrous results for the organization. We have seen that one example of a fixed cost is salaries. Others are financing charges, rents, business rates, heating and depreciation.

As we have seen, variable costs include the materials used in making a product or providing a service. They also include any labour cost that is charged at an hourly rate for that job or service. These variable costs are relatively easy to control because they can be readily identified and action can be taken to correct the situation if they are seen to be moving in an unexpected way.

Semi-variable costs behave as though they are a combination of fixed and variable costs, with an element that is fixed and an element that alters with the level of activity. An example of such a cost would be maintenance, which has a planned fixed element whatever the level of activity and a variable element which alters with activity. Such costs are extremely difficult to identify.

Example 19

We can now study an example illustrating the use of absorption costing through the medium of a manufacturing organization which has two departments and a single product. During manufacture the product spends some time in each of the departments. The expected costs for a month are:

	£
Business rates	300
Heating and lighting	60
Depreciation	100
Salaries	6,000
Administration	400

The resources allocated to the two departments are:

Department	A	B
Floor area (square metres)	20	40
Number of employees	5	15
Value of machinery (£000)	40	10
Production labour hours	600	1,800

In order to calculate the amount that must be charged out by the departments for work done, the appropriate overhead cost has to be established. This is calculated by first of all apportioning the overhead costs to the departments on an equitable basis:

Cost	Department A	Department B	Total	Basis of apportionment
	£	£	£	
Rates	100	200	300	Floor area
Heating and lighting	15	45	60	Number of employees
Depreciation	80	20	100	Value of machinery
Salaries	1,500	4,500	6,000	Labour hours
Administration	100	300	400	Number of employees
Total	£1,795	£5,065	£6,860	

The total overhead allocated to the departments is: department A, £1,795, department B, £5,065. It is now necessary to decide how the overheads are to be recovered. One way of doing it would be to calculate the amount of overhead to be charged for each labour hour of work done. To do this it is necessary to divide the overheads allocated to the department by the number of production labour hours expected in the department. Using the example, we have:

Department	A	B
Total overheads allocated (£)	1,795	5,065
Production labour hours	600	1,800
Labour hour rate (£)	2.99	2.81

This is an acceptable approach, but it is by no means the only one. Overheads can be charged at a rate per machine hour or as a percentage of the production wages. However they are charged, this approach will help to ensure that overhead costs are not overlooked when prices are calculated. In order to price a job that is expected to spend two labour hours in department A and one in department B and which would incur matrial costs of £200 and a wage rate of £6 per hour, it is necessary to carry out the following calculation:

	£
Materials	200
Labour: A 2 × £6	12
B 1 × £6	6
Prime or direct cost	218

Add the fixed/overhead cost:

Department A: 2 × £2.99	5.98
Department B: 1 × £2.81	2.81
	226.79

£226.79 is simply the cost of the job. Any profit that was required would have to be added to it. The basis on which the overheads have been allocated with the reasons for the choice are as follows.

Rates. Based on floor area, because this is the usual method of charging rates. Department B has twice the floor area of department A, so the rates are allocated on a basis of two to one, i.e. two-thirds of £300 = £200 to department B and one-third of £300 = £100 to department A.

Heating and lighting. Based on the number of employees, but production labour hours could have been used just as well. Department B has three times as many employees as department A, so heating and lighting are allocated on the basis of three to one, i.e. three-quarters of £60 = £45 to department B and a quarter of £60 = £15 to department A.

Depreciation. Based on the value of machinery. Department A's machinery is four times as valuable as department B's, so depreciation is allocated on the basis of four to one, i.e. four-fifths of £100 = £80 goes to department A and one-fifth of £100 = £20 to department B.

Salaries. Based on the number of labour hours, but the number of employees could have just as easily been used. Department B's production labour hours are three times those of department A, so salaries are allocated on the basis of three to one, i.e. three-quarters of £6,000 = £4,500 goes to department B and one-quarter of £6,000 = £1,500 to department A.

Administration. See if you can calculate this one for yourself and check with the answer given on page 120.

We already have seen that organizations usually have large indirect or overhead costs that are not charged directly to the service or product that is being provided. It is necessary to recover all of these costs if an undertaking is to be seen to be running efficiently or making a profit. Any organization that employs only the direct costs in arriving at the cost of a service or product will soon cease to exist or else become a drain on the resources of the community.

If, for example, a service organization provided a simple service and consisted of three departments it would be possible for it to charge what it considered to be a good rate to its customers and find at the end of the year that it was making a loss. This can be illustrated in the following example.

Example 20

Good Service Ltd has three departments and its expected costs and activity for the next year are:

Personnel Department annual fixed costs	£120,000
Finance Department annual fixed costs	£100,000
Service Department annual fixed costs	£90,000
Service Department variable costs £40 per hour	
Hours of service to be sold during the year 5,000	
Charge to customers per hour £100	

Ignoring the fixed costs of the Personnel and Finance departments, a charge of £100 per hour seems to be adequate to give a reasonable profit.

	£	£
Income 5,000 hours at £100 per hour		500,000
Expenses		
Fixed costs of Service Department	90,000	
Variable costs: 5,000 hours at £40 per hour	200,000	290,000
Profit		210,000

It is only when the costs of the other two departments are considered that it becomes apparent that a loss of £10,000 has been incurred. This is calculated as:

	£	£
Surplus from Service Department		210,000
Less		
Fixed cost of Personnel Department	120,000	
Fixed cost of Finance Department	100,000	220,000
Loss		10,000

In order to avoid this situation it is necessary to find the total charge per hour to ensure that all costs are recovered, together with any profit the company requires. The way to achieve this is first to calculate the charge per hour needed to recover the fixed costs. That is the total fixed costs divided by the hours of service you expect to sell.

$$\frac{£120,000 + £100,000 + £90,000}{5,000 \text{ hours}} = \frac{£310,000}{5,000 \text{ hours}} = £62 \text{ per hour}$$

If there is to be any profit this will require an additional cost per hour to the customers. Good Service Ltd requires £40,000 p.a. profit, which necessitates an additional hourly charge of

$$\frac{£40,000}{5,000 \text{ hours}} = £8 \text{ per hour}$$

The charge per hour now becomes:

	£
Variable cost per hour	40
Add fixed costs per hour	62
Add profit per hour	8
	110

The 5,000 hours of service earn:

$$5,000 \times £110 = £550,000$$

The costs incurred are:

Fixed costs:	£	£
Service Department	90,000	
Personnel Department	120,000	
Finance Department	100,000	310,000
Surplus		240,000
Less variable cost 5,000 hrs × £40		200,000
Profit		40,000

In order to explore this a little further let us assume that the total overheads of Poor Real Ltd are £620,000 which are to be allocated to the Personnel Department, Finance Department and Service Department on an equitable basis. There are many ways in which this can be done which include percentage of direct wages, labour hour rate, machine hour rate and number of employees. The number of employees in each of the departments is:

Personnel department	Service department	Finance department
15	12	13

Using this information to apportion the overheads to the three departments we share the £620,000 overheads as follows:

Personnel Department $\frac{15}{40}$ × £620,000 = £232,500

Service Department $\frac{12}{40}$ × £620,000 = £186,000

Finance departments $\frac{13}{40}$ × £62,000 = £201,500

Total as an accuracy check   £620,000

This means that if the organization is to avoid incurring a loss the Personnel Department must earn £232,500, the Service Department £186,000 and the Finance Department £201,500; otherwise, as is usually the case, the Service Department must earn enough to ensure that all the organization's overheads are recovered.

The apportionment of overheads to departments is a major source of organizational controversy. The Personnel Manager who unexpectedly finds that the department has had £232,500 of overheads charged to it is not going to be at all pleased, particularly as these are costs over which he or she has little or no control. The most effective approach is to tackle the person responsible for the allocation of the overheads and ascertain the basis on which it has been done. You may then be able to challenge the allocation and be responsible for a more appropriate figure.

In this chapter we have been considering the traditional absorption methods of allocating overheads, but some people consider that these no longer provide good information for decision making and control. This concern has encouraged another method of allocating overheads to be developed, called Activity Based Costing, sometimes referred to as ABC. It is felt to give relevant information to management quickly and so help with decision making and control. The two methods may be compared diagrammatically in figures 10 and 11.

Figure 10
Absorption costing

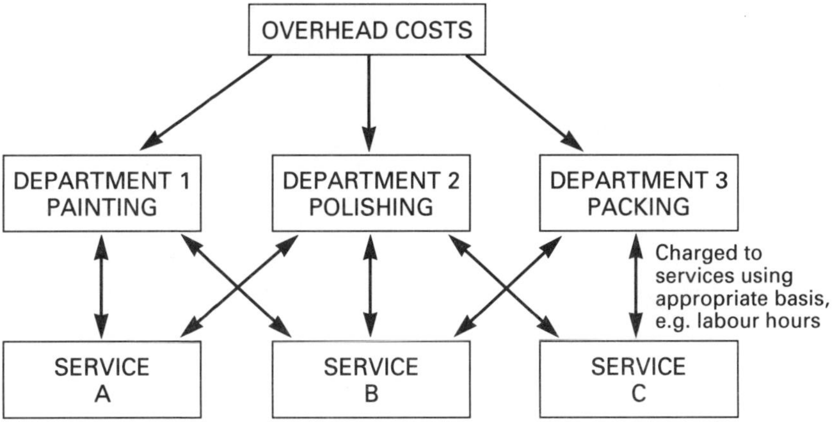

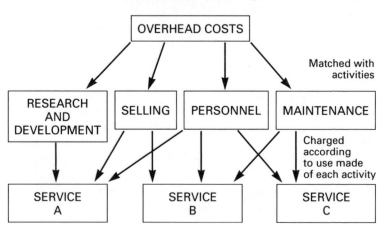

Figure 11
Activity based costing

Chapter 13

Standard Costing

Standard costing is extremely important to personnel managers as it can be used to provide a guide to the expected cost of each training programme offered or each member of staff recruited. These can then be compared with the actual costs incurred to help ensure that the department is well managed and that costs are properly controlled. Indeed, the system is critical to the efficiency of the organization as a whole.

The standard cost is the expected cost per unit, and it is derived from a mixture of historical information and forecasting techniques. The more information that is available the more accurate the standard is likely to be, but it is important to remember that it is a forecast and will therefore rarely, if ever, be absolutely correct.

Once the standard has been set, it is crucially important to compare the actual result with the expected result, at least monthly but preferably more often, and where they differ significantly to ensure that remedial action is taken promptly.

It is here that a good management information system can be extremely helpful. Most organizations are complex, and people in them receive an enormous amount of information, often in the form of computer print-outs. If there are a great number of items that differ from the standard, it will not be possible to correct and report on each one, so two things are necessary.

First, an acceptable difference between the standard and actual results must be decided upon. It will vary from organization to organization but it may be, for example, that anything within ±15 per cent of plan is accepted, whilst anything outside that range has to be reported upon and corrected. Secondly, the system should then ensure that anything outside the ±15 per cent range is highlighted, perhaps by means of an asterisk, so that the person responsible for correcting the situation is made aware of it and takes the necessary action.

Setting standards

When a standard costing system is established it should be remembered that it has tremendous potential for good or ill. If people feel that it is being foisted upon them without consultation, they will be suspicious and resentful and may cause the system to falter. On the other hand, if they feel that they have been consulted from the beginning and their ideas have been considered, they will feel involved and will want the system to succeed. In setting the standard or expected cost, too, a great deal of care must be taken. Broadly there are three approaches which are commonly used.

Perfect standard

This assumes that people in an organization can work at peak efficiency throughout the working year. It is, in fact, an impossible target to achieve. The effect on morale is devastating, and eventually the workforce will become totally demotivated, having gone through a cycle from being well motivated and determined to make the system work to disillusioned failure, with no faith in the management of the organization. Having been involved in the discussion, people will work hard to meet the targets, but as they fail to reach them week after week their enthusiasm will wane until the realization sets in that it is no good trying because the targets cannot be met.

Slack standard

This assumes that people do not enjoy being faced with a challenge and would prefer to spend their time talking and doing crosswords than have a demanding job that gives satisfaction through achievement. The target having been set, people will work hard to achieve it, but once they realize that it can be reached week after week with little effort, attention will wander and work will become slipshod. Once again disillusionment will set in as the feeling grows that the organization neither values its work force nor understands its capabilities.

Attainable standard

This assumes that people become well motivated and will do their best if they are involved in decisions and given tasks that stretch them but can be achieved. In setting the standard, the starting point is past performance. The standards for previous years are studied, and any scope for improvement within achievable limits is built into the standard for the next year. Consultation should take place with the staff responsible for achieving the standard, to obtain their support, and this should help to ensure a well-motivated workforce working to good standards of performance. Where possible, those who consistently achieve above average results should be rewarded in some way, so that people are constantly stimulated to perform well. Realistically, however, it is not always possible to reward good performance.

Elements of cost

Costs break down into three elements: labour, materials and overheads, which consist of such items as rates, depreciation and the salaries of 'non-productive' workers. Here 'non-productive' means those who are not directly making the goods or providing the service, and standards have to be set for each of them. The detailed control of overhead costs is outside the scope of this book, and the rest of this chapter will deal with the control of labour and material costs, the ones that can most readily be changed in the short term.

Labour costs

The expected labour cost of a job or operation can be arrived at by going through the process of reaching an attainable standard (see above). Once it has been set, it is not usually possible to alter a standard very often; in fact it is rarely altered more than once or twice a year. The following illustrations will help to explain the way in which labour costs are controlled, using the labour rate variance and the labour efficiency variance.

Labour rate variance. Caused by changes in rates of pay, and calculated using the formula:

Actual hours × Change in wage rate per hour

The change in wage rate per hour is the standard wage rate minus the actual wage rate.

Labour efficiency variance. Caused by changes in the speed of production, and calculated using the formula:

Standard wage rate per hour $\times$ Change in the hours worked

The change in the hours worked is the standard hours minus the actual hours.

Example 21

The standard cost of labour is four hours at £7 per hour—£28 per unit. The actual cost is:

380 hours at £7.50 per hour = £2,850 per 100 units = £28.50 per unit

The labour rate variance is:

$$380 \times 50p = £190$$

When costs are greater than the standard the difference between the budgeted and actual cost is termed an adverse variance. The variance is the difference between the expected and the actual cost, and it is adverse because it is more than expected. Had the cost been less than expected, the variance would have been favourable. It must be emphasized that a favourable variance is as bad as an adverse one, since both indicate a failure to work to plan and may need corrective action. The labour rate variance is adverse because the rate has increased from £7 to £7.50 per hour.

The labour efficiency variance is:

$$£7(400 - 380) = £140 \text{ favourable}$$

The variance is favourable because for 100 units you would expect to use 400 hours but only 380 hours have been used; so the total labour variance is £190 adverse and £140 favourable, which nets down to £50 (£190 − £140) adverse. This can be confirmed by comparing the actual labour cost of £2,850 with the expected labour cost of £2,800 (400 hours at £7 per hour), which confirms the total variance of £50 adverse. It therefore shows the calculations of the individual labour variances to be correct.

Material costs

The process described for setting an attainable standard above will give
the expected material cost of a job or operation, which enables material
costs to be controlled through the medium of the material price and
material usage variances illustrated below.

Material price variance. Caused by changes in the purchase price of
the materials used, and calculated by using the formula:

Actual quantity × Change in price

The change in price is the standard minus the actual price.

Material usage variance. Caused by changes in the quantity of materials used, and calculated by using the formula:

Standard price × Change in use

The change in use is the standard minus the actual use.

Example 22

The standard material price and usage cost is 20m of material at £8 a
metre—£160 per unit. The actual cost is:

2,400m of material at £7.60 a metre = £18,240 per 100 units
= £182.40 per unit

The material price variance is:

2,400 (£8 – £7.60) = £960 favourable.

The material price is favourable because the price has fallen from £8 a
metre to £7.60 a metre.

The material usage variance is:

£8 (2,000 – 2,400) = £3,200 adverse

The material usage variance is adverse because the usage has increased
from 2,000m to 2,400m.

This enables the total materials variance to be calculated from the

£960 favourable variance and the £3,200 adverse variance, giving a net variance of £2,240 adverse. This can be confirmed by comparing the actual material cost of £18,240 with the expected material cost of £16,000 (2000m × £8 a metre), which confirms the total material variance of £2,240 adverse, and shows the calculation of the individual material variances to be correct.

Corrective action

Having calculated the variances and found them to be outside the parameters that are acceptable to the organization, the information system should flag them in some distinctive way so that the person responsible is made aware that action is necessary. Some possible causes and suggested actions to correct the labour and material variances follow.

Labour rate variance

1. Bad estimate. Accepted as an explainable variance until a new standard can be set.
2. Nationally agreed change in wage rates. Accept until a new standard can be set.
3. Using more or less highly skilled people than are needed to carry out the operation. Make the necessary change in the people carrying out the work, and discuss with the supervisor/manager.

Labour efficiency variance

1. Bad estimate. Accept until the standard can be changed.
2. Using more or less highly skilled people than planned for. Make the necessary changes and have discussions with those responsible.
3. Poor morale among staff. A serious problem for the Personnel Department, which will have to discover the cause and if possible rectify it; failing all else, people may have to be asked to leave.

Material price variance

1. Bad estimate. Accept until the standard can be changed.

2. Internationally agreed price change. Accept until the standard can be changed.
3. Using material of a better or worse quality than needed. Make the necessary change in the material used and investigate with the purchasing section.

Material usage variance

1. Bad estimate. Accept until the standard can be changed.
2. Quality of material. Investigate with purchasing section and take necessary action.
3. Labour efficiency. Explore with Personnel and correct as quickly as possible.

A good system of standard costing is invaluable to management in helping to ensure that an organization is adhering to its planned course and things are not getting out of control. The Personnel Manager who understands costing will not only be better able to control the costs of his or her department and demonstrate its effective management, but will also be able to assist in other areas, especially where variances in labour costs can be attributed to a mismatch between people's skills and their functions.

Work through exercises 12–14 and compare your answers with the suggested ones given.

Exercise 12

A service organization has the following standard costs per day for the service it provides: labour, 8 hours at £40 per hour; materials, 5 litres at £15 per litre; overheads, £60 per day. The actual costs for one week of five days are: labour, 38 hours at £41 per hour; materials, 28 litres at £14.50 per litre; overheads, £340. Calculate the variances and comment on their use.

Exercise 13

The Personnel Department is responsible for providing a one-week 40-hour induction programme for new recruits. The standard costs of the programme are: hourly salary per recruit, £7.20; hourly salary per

134   *Finance and Accounting for Managers*

trainer, £8.65; overhead costs per week for the Personnel Department, £1,000. The actual costs of a training week for 20 delegates are:

                                                                        £
42 hours training for 20 recruits with salaries of £7 per hour   5,880·00
42 hours training by 2 trainers with salaries of £8.70 per hour   730·80
Overheads   1,200·00
                                                                  7,810·80

Calculate the relevant variances and comment on their use to the Personnel Manager.

Exercise 14

Explain the main factors of standard costing that make it an effective control tool for personnel managers.

Solution 12

Standard cost for one week of five days:

Labour	8 × £40 × 5 =	£1,600
Materials	5 × £15 × 5 =	375
Overheads	£60 × 5 =	300
		£2,275

Actual cost for one week of five days:

Labour	38 × £41 =	£1,558
Materials	28 × £14.50 =	406
Overheads	=	300
		£2,304

Total variance:

$$£2,304 - £2,275 = £29 \text{ adverse}$$

This represents only 1 per cent of budget and would in practice probably not be investigated further, because of time constraints, but we will calculate the individual variances that go to make up the £29.

Labour variances:

Standard cost	£1,600
Actual cost	1,558
	£ 42 favourable

This breaks down into the following labour rate and labour efficiency variances:

Labour rate variance 38 hours × (£40 – £41)   £38 adverse

Labour efficiency variance £40 × (£40 – 38) hours   £80 favourable
which nets back to the total labour variance: £42 favourable

Material variances:

Standard cost	£375
Actual cost	406
	£ 31 adverse

This breaks down into the following material price and material usage variances:

Material price variance 28 × (£15 – £14.50)   £14 favourable

Material usage variance £15 × (25 – 28)   £45 adverse
which nets back to the total materials variance   £31 adverse

Overhead variance:

This can be dealt with only in total:

Standard cost	£300
Actual cost	340
	£ 40 adverse

Each of these variances should then be discussed in turn and suggestions made as to the most appropriate course of action.

Solution 13

	£
Standard cost of a week for 20 recruits	
Recruits 20 × £7.20 × 40 =	5,760·00
Trainers 2 × £8.65 x 40 =	692·00
Overheads	1,000·00
	7,452·00
Actual cost of a week for 20 delegates	7,810·80
Adverse variance	358·80

This variance represents 4.8% of standard or accepted cost and may therefore be considered to be within accepted tolerances. However let us undertake a further investigation. The variances will involve only labour and overheads as there are no materials that have been separately costed.

	£
Actual cost of recruits	5,880
Standard cost of recruits	5,760
Adverse variance	120

Labour rate variance:

Actual hours × change in rate	
(20 × 42) × 20p =	168 favourable

Labour efficiency variance:

Standard wage per hour × change in hours	
£7.20 × (2 × 20)	288·00 adverse
	120·00 adverse

Actual cost of trainers	730·80
Standard cost of trainers	692·00
Adverse variance	38·80

Labour rate variance:

(2 × 42) × 5p =	4·20 adverse

Labour efficiency variance:

£8.65 × (2 × 2) =	34·60 adverse
	38·80 adverse

Overhead variance:

$$\frac{\text{Standard} - \text{actual overheads}}{1,000 - 1,200} = \quad \begin{array}{c} £ \\ 200 \end{array} \quad \text{adverse}$$

Total variance:

Labour—trainers	adverse	38·80
Labour—recruits	adverse	120·00
Overheads	adverse	200·00
	adverse	358·80

Solution 14

Points that should be considered include:

- Preparation of the planned or standard level of activity
- Comparison of the actual activity with the planned activity
- The significance of any variances obtained
- The cause of the variance
- Decisions on any necesssary corrective action
- Quick and effective action.

Chapter 14

Marginal Costing and Personnel Decisions

We have so far been concerned with ensuring that all costs are accounted for and recovered. There is also an approach to costing that focuses attention on those costs that will be altered by a particular decision, in order to emphasize the impact of that decision. This approach is called marginal costing and whilst it is not a complete system it is of enormous help to the Personnel Manager when making decisions, for example, about selling, training or consultancy services (whether within or outside the organization).

Under marginal costing the fixed costs, like depreciation, salaries and interest charges, are considered to have been set as a matter of policy and to remain fixed within given parameters for the period under review. This is not to say that the fixed costs are not important. For most organizations they constitute the bulk of the costs incurred and to ignore them completely would be a recipe for disaster. But they can be regarded as not directly affecting a decision that is being made. The marginal cost can be described as the cost of one more unit, be it a product or service, and the difference between these two costs can be graphically illustrated in figures 12 and 13.

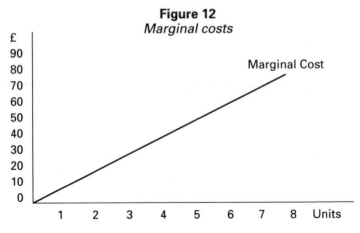

Figure 12
Marginal costs

138

Figure 13

Fixed costs

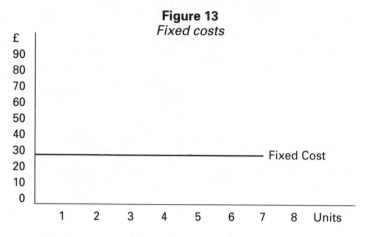

The marginal cost line starts at zero because if nothing is being done—no service provided or units made—no marginal cost is being incurred, whereas the fixed cost line is parallel to the base because the cost is the same whether one unit or eight units of product or service is being provided.

Marginal costing employs the important concept of contribution. Contribution is the selling price per unit of service or product minus the marginal cost per unit of providing it. The contribution goes first towards meeting the fixed costs of the organization and then provided the contribution is large enough it becomes profit. If the contribution is not enough to meet the fixed costs a loss is incurred, as can be seen in the following illustration.

Example 23

The Personnel Department offers training, for which it charges £100 per hour for up to 20 delegates. The marginal costs have been calculated at £70 per hour and the fixed costs for the period are £9,990. The manager needs to know the contribution per hour, how many hours of training must be sold to break even (i.e. make neither a profit nor a loss), and what the profit or loss would be if 350 hours of training were sold.

The contribution per hour is the selling price per hour minus the marginal cost per hour:

$$£100 - £70 = £30$$

The number of hours that must be sold in order to break even is:

$$\frac{\text{Fixed costs}}{\text{Contribution per hour}} = \frac{£9,990}{30} = 333 \text{ hours}$$

The profit or loss if 350 hours of training are sold is the total contribution minus the fixed costs:

$$£10,500 \ (£30 \times 350 \text{ hours}) - £9,990 = £510$$

Let us look at another example of how this concept is used:

Example 24

A personnel consultancy organization has fixed costs of £60,000, marginal costs of £50 per unit and a selling price of £150 per unit. Each unit that is sold contributes £100 to the fixed costs, and once these have been met the contribution is to profit. This can be further shown as:

Units Sold	Contributions (£)	Fixed Costs (£)	Profit (or loss) (£)	
0	0	60,000	(60,000)	
1	100	60,000	(59,900)	
2	200	60,000	(59,800)	
3	300	60,000	(59,700)	
599	59,900	60,000	(100)	
600	60,000	60,000	(0)	break even
601	60,100	60,000	100	

At 600 units the organization breaks even. More than 600 units results in a profit, and less in a loss. The break-even point in units sold can be calculated by applying the formula:

$$\frac{\text{Total fixed costs}}{\text{Selling price} - \text{fixed cost per unit}}$$

which in our example gives:

$$\frac{60,000}{(150 - 50)} = \frac{60,000}{100} = 600 \text{ units}$$

The relationship may be shown graphically (see figure 14) if we assume the information previously given applies and the maximum possible number of units than can be sold is 700.

Figure 14
Break-even point

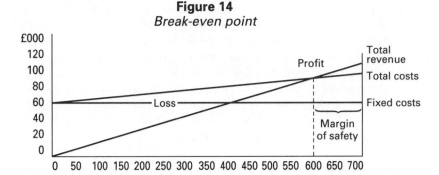

The horizontal axis represents activity, in this case the units sold, and the vertical axis the value in terms of both costs and revenue. The horizontal axis goes to the maximum possible level of activity, and at this point a vertical line is drawn, which shows where all the lines of the graph end. The vertical axis must go up to the total sales or the total costs, whichever is the greater. The total revenue is obtained by multiplying the total units sold by the selling price per unit.

$$700 \times 150 = £105,000$$

A mark is made on the vertical line opposite the £105,000. This is then joined to the zero to give the total revenue line. The total cost is calculated by adding the fixed cost to the total marginal cost, which in this case is:

(marginal cost per unit $\times$ units sold) + fixed costs = (£50 $\times$ 700) + £60,000 = £35,000 + £60,000 = £95,000.

A mark is made on the vertical axis opposite the £95,000 and joined to the fixed costs of £60,000 to give the total cost line. The break-even point is where the total cost and total revenue lines intercept. Anything to the left of it represents loss; anything to the right of it, profit.

Contribution is used by many organizations in an attempt to ensure that spare capacity is fully employed at off-peak times. British Rail, bus companies, BT, the electricity undertakings, British Airways and hotel chains are among those that have high fixed costs and employ a two- or multi-tier pricing system in order to persuade the public to use their services at off-peak times. Every extra contribution that is received helps to meet the enormous fixed costs they carry and either reduces losses or increases profits. Full rates are charged at peak periods but at off-peak times bargain offers are made. For example, British Rail charges over £30 return from Portsmouth to Waterloo at peak times but reduces it to £15.70 at off-peak times. Provided they are receiving more in fares than it is costing to run the train, they are receiving a contribution to their enormous fixed costs.

We have seen that there are several costing methods available to the Personnel Manager. The one you choose should meet your needs and provide you with relevant information to manage yourself and your department more effectively. Decisions based on incomplete or inappropriate information are bad decisions. To be successful it is essential to have the right information in the right place at the right time.

Exercise 15

Look at example 23. What would you recommend should be done if demand for training fell to 300 hours? What would be the magnitude of the loss?

Exercise 16

The Personnel Department markets its services in recruitment consultancy. The marginal cost has been calculated to be £19,500 per managerial appointment and the charge to the customers is £25,000 per appointment. The relevant fixed costs are £319,000 and it is expected that 70 managerial recruitments will be undertaken for clients. Draw the break-even chart for the above information and read from the chart the results of the planned 70 recruits.

Exercise 17

Enumerate three ways in which the concept of contribution is of help to personnel managers.

Exercise 18

Your Managing Director is reviewing training costs with a view to possibly purchasing training from consultants rather than employing your department. The costs of buying in training for the standard induction programme would be £4,000 for up to 20 delegates. The costs charged by your department are £6,000 for up to 20 delegates. The overheads charged to the department from head office are £10,000 and they are recovered in the quoted costs over four programmes. How would you demonstrate to the Managing Director that your department's costs are lower than those of the outside consultant?

Solution 15

If demand fell to 300 hours, the loss would be:

$$(333 \text{ hours} - 300 \text{ hours}) \times 30 = £990$$

This is less than the loss involved in doing nothing which would be £9,990. In the short run it is therefore better to keep going and look to save costs, increase prices or find new outlets.

Solution 16

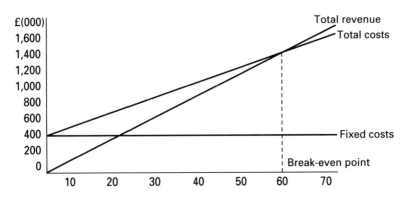

The break-even point is at 58 units sold.

Total revenue 70 × £25,000 =	£1,750,000
Total cost is £319,000 + (19,500 x 70) =	£1,684,000
Profit	£66,000

Solution 17

1. Recruitment
2. Training
3. Establishing Departmental Contribution

Solution 18

True cost of buying in	£4,000
Add 25% of £10,000	£2,500
	£6,500

Therefore the Personnel Department is cheaper, as the £10,000 head office costs have to be found, whether you buy in or not.

Chapter 15

The Planning System

A chart of the planning system is shown in figure 15.

Figure 15
The planning system

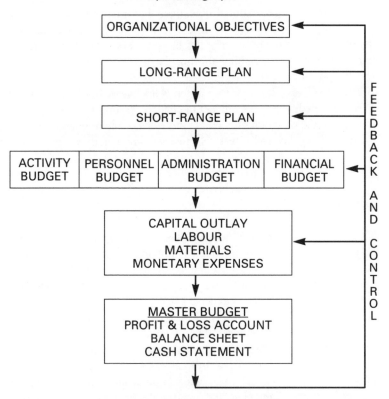

In following this model we see that the first purpose of the planning system is to ensure that organizational objectives are set. This is usually undertaken by the top executives of the organization and would normally include the Chief Executive together with his or her deputy, the Personnel Director, the Financial Director and the Marketing Director. Other people may be co-opted on to the team as they are required but it is usual to keep the group to a workable size whenever possible. In setting the objectives the team will have regard to the past performance of the organization, particularly over the last two or three years, as well as the likely events of the next five years or so which will have an impact on it. In doing this they will consider reports from people who are in touch with the customers so that any changes in customer profile can be quickly identified. The latest economic forecasts will be considered, together with population trends and expected changes in fashion and technology. There are a great many different organizational objectives that might be set, including such things as providing the fastest service, being most concerned about the environment, having the largest market share, having the happiest employees, making the biggest profit or making the most reliable product.

The objectives may be for up to ten years ahead, but it is important to remember that they are subject to change. No organization survives for long in the current highly competitive environment unless it is able to respond quickly and effectively to changing conditions, but objectives do set a course that the organization is able to follow.

Long-range plan

This is drawn up to enable the objectives to be achieved and will probably cover the next ten years, but it is important to remember that it is virtually impossible to plan accurately so far into the future. The first year will be relatively firm and years 2–3 should be fairly accurate unless something totally unexpected occurs, like 'Black Monday' in October 1987 when the stock market collapsed. Years 4 and 5 will be rather less certain and years 6–10 pretty tentative, except perhaps in the case of large projects which require extensive capital outlay. The long-range plan will be adjusted year by year as a result of feedback as to its feasibility, once it has been expressed in financial terms in the master budget. The long-range plan, and in particular the early years of it, will see a great deal of in-fighting as each manager stakes a claim for as large a share of the budget 'cake' as possible. Personalities will be very much to the fore, and there is a real danger that unless there is a good system with a reasonable approach the most aggressive character will receive far more than his or her entitlement.

Short-range plan

This will be the budget for the next twelve months and before it is finished, consultation will ideally have taken place at all levels of the organization. Without the opportunity to be involved in the preparation of the budget, people will feel that it has been imposed on them and be resentful. If, on the other hand, they feel that they have contributed to its preparation they are more likely to feel involved and supportive, so that the chances of the plan being adhered to will be greatly enhanced.

The budget works in the same way as standard costing, the difference being in scale. Whereas standard costing refers to a job, operation, section or department, budgetary control encompasses the whole organization, but uses exactly the same technique as standard costing. Actual performance is compared with planned performances on a weekly, monthly or quarterly basis, and significant differences are reported upon so that corrective action can be taken.

The budgets

The short-range plan feeds into the detailed budgets discussed below, which are firm for the first year but become more tentative the further they go into the future. With all planning it is important to be flexible and to allow for the unexpected, as things will change, and attempts to treat a budget as set in tablets of stone, under no circumstances to be altered, will cause more problems than they solve.

Activity budget

This consists of the expected hours of service that an organization believes it can provide in the period that is being planned for, or units it can produce, or jobs it can complete. It will be based on the information—provided by market research carried out by the organization's employees or bought in—as to the likely level of demand. The information will have to be handled with care, as there is a danger that people will want to paint an optimistic picture and may unintentionally overstate the level of demand. To help counteract this, it is a good idea to obtain information from as many sources as possible and to prepare three levels of activity, most pessimistic, most optimistic and most likely. This will help to minimize the risk of people getting carried away with their own enthusiasm.

Having set the budget, it is essential to monitor it closely to ensure that errors are quickly noticed and the relevant corrections made. Bad planning here will have an impact throughout the whole organization, as will be discussed later in this chapter.

Personnel budget

In order to meet the level of demand anticipated by the activity budget it is essential to ensure that enough people of the right calibre are available throughout the organization. To achieve this effective recruitment systems have to be in place, reinforced by job analysis and training programmes. It is both fashionable and necessary for both the public and private sectors to operate lean and healthy organizations, and for them to succeed the people must operate effectively.

The fast-changing environment in which we all operate means that the people must be flexible in this approach and constantly retrained to keep up with current developments. The Personnel Manager has a key role in ensuring that the requirements of staff for development are identified and met. Failure to achieve this will lead first to a demotivated team because staff will feel that they are not performing effectively and then to the possible demise of the organization because it fails to compete with more efficient people.

Administration budget

Built around the expected level of activity, this budget will ensure that the correct administration systems are in place with suitably experienced and/or qualified people to enable the organization to meet the demands that are placed upon it. Obtaining the right person to meet the particular needs of a section or department is an extremely specialized matter, and recruitment consultants are frequently called in, particularly for the more senior positions. Good administration can help ensure the successful implementation of plans, so this budget should be capable of providing the necessary resources to meet the organization's needs.

Financial budget

The financial budget is based on the activity budget, and is used to ensure that there are sufficient financial resources for the plan to be met. Organizations need resources of materials, labour and money to enable them to operate, and a shortage of any one of these will cause plans to fail. Finance is used in every area, as are people and materials, but there is a danger that the financial implications of plans or actions may sometimes be overlooked. The preparation of the financial budget helps to ensure that this does not happen, as every manager is involved and the accountant's role, contrary to popular belief, is simply to clothe their ideas in monetary terms.

In the past some accountants have been seen as unapproachable people; speaking a strange language, whose main purpose in life was to say no, closely followed by a desire to confuse. This is now changing and the accountant is seen more as an organizational resource, a person who can give valuable advice on a great many matters.

Capital outlay budget

Capital outlay involves heavy expenditure on such fixed assets as land and buildings, plant and machinery or fixtures and fittings, which may be spent in one year, but may also involve large capital programmes spread over several years. Examples would be a new housing estate, a land reclamation scheme, a drainage system, a sports complex or the development of a commercial dock. The capital budget, unlike the revenue budgets, often involves heavy expenditure spread over several years and should therefore receive close scrutiny before any schemes are finally approved. Various methods are available and they are described in chapter 18.

Materials budget

This is prepared in order to ensure that sufficient materials are available to meet the anticipated demand, whilst at the same time enabling the organization to avoid tying up too much money in unnecessarily high stocks of material. The level will depend on the forecast in the activity budget, but it should be borne in mind that more and more organizations are attempting to use the 'just in time' method of inventory control. In practice it is extremely difficult to achieve, as much depends on the reliability of the supplier, with any small delay causing enormous problems.

Cash budget

This is a more sensitive version of the financial budget which concentrates on the day-to-day movements of money in the organization. It is complementary to the financial budget, and draws on the activity and other budgets. Properly monitored, the cash budget can be extremely helpful in controlling the activities of the organization and avoiding embarrassing short-term cash-flow problems. The subject is dealt with in chapter 16.

Expenses budget

This covers the expected level of such items of expense as rates, heating and lighting, telephones, postage, stationery and canteen costs. Most of them will be known with a reasonable degree of certainty, at least for the next year, and, whilst they have to be integrated with the other budgets, they are not so directly changed by differing levels of activity.

Master budget

The master budget clothes these ideas in monetary terms to see whether they are in fact feasible when measured against planned levels of profitability and liquidity. If it shows that there will be a loss instead of a profit, or too little money will be generated, the information will be fed back into the system and the process restarted.

None of the budgets mentioned can stand on its own, and each depends on the others. It is no use planning to provide 10,000 hours of service if you only have enough people to give 7,000 hours, or to produce 50,000 units if you are only able to sell 40,000. To avoid mismatching of this sort, organizations have to decide what their limiting factor is, that is to say, which of the budgets is most restricted, either through shortage of resources or because of a lack of demand. Once identified, the limiting factor becomes the starting point of the budget, and all the others are built around it. An organization may decide that it can meet any level of demand, and if this is so, then the activity or sales budget will be the starting point and all the other budgets will be dependent on it, as illustrated in figure 16. This shows an integrated system of budgeting in which each budget has an impact on the others, but the one that restricts the overall budgets in this case is the activity/sales budget, as the organization feels that, whatever the demand, it has the resources to meet it.

Figure 16
Limiting factor activity/sales budget

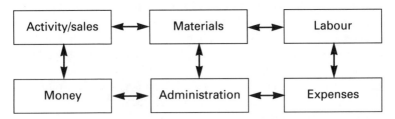

The system is as appropriate for the public sector as it is for the private sector but the limiting factor in the public sector is frequently money and so the model would be as in figure 17.

Figure 17
Limiting factor cash budget

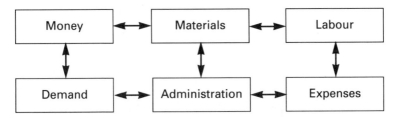

Exercise 19

Prepare a model of your organization's planning system and compare it
with the one illustrated in this chapter. What do you consider to be its
strengths and weaknesses? What is the Personnel Manager's contribution to the planning system? Identify the main items of income and
expenditure for which she or he is responsible.

Draw up the plan or budget for the Personnel Department for the
coming year. If you do not know how much money will be involved
for each item simply list the headings involved.

Exercise 20

An organization has budgeted sales for three months (twelve weeks) of
600 units at £20 each. The material bought and used will be 300lb at
60p a pound. The labour cost will be 360 hours at £15 per hour and
other expenses £40 per week. The cash in hand at the start of the period
is £400. Customers receive one month's credit, and suppliers and other
expenses are paid on time. Draw up the sales, materials, labour,
expenses and cash budgets for the three months and the budgeted profit
and loss account and balance sheet. No money was due from customers. At the beginning of the three months, there was 10lb of material
in hand and £406 capital.

Solution 20

Sales Budget
Units sold

Week	Plan	Actual	Cumulative	Actual
1	50		50	
2	50		100	
3	50		150	
4	50		200	
5	50		250	
6	50		300	
7	50		350	
8	50		400	
9	50		450	
10	50		500	
11	50		550	
12	50		600	

Labour budget

Week	Planned hours	Actual hours	Planned hours	Actual hours
1	30		30	
2	30		60	
3	30		90	
4	30		120	
5	30		150	
6	30		180	
7	30		210	
8	30		240	
9	30		270	
10	30		300	
11	30		330	
12	30		360	

Expenses Budget

Week	Planned	Actual	Cumulative Planned	Cumulative Actual
1	£40		£ 40	
2	40		80	
3	40		120	
4	40		160	
5	40		200	
6	40		240	
7	40		280	
8	40		320	
9	40		360	
10	40		400	
11	40		440	
12	40		480	

Materials budget

Week	Opening balance		Purchases				Use			Closing balance	
	Plan	Actual	Plan	Cum.	Actual	Cum.	Plan	Cum.	Actual	Plan	Actual
1	10		25	25			25	25		10	
2	10		25	50			25	50		10	
3	10		25	75			25	75		10	
4	10		25	100			25	100		10	
5	10		25	125			25	125		10	
6	10		25	150			25	150		10	
7	10		25	175			25	175		10	
8	10		25	200			25	200		10	
9	10		25	225			25	225		10	
10	10		25	250			25	250		10	
11	10		25	275			25	275		10	
12	10		25	300			25	300		10	

Cash budget

Week:	1	2	3	4	5	6	7	8	9	10	11	12
Opening balance	£400	(£105)	(£610)	(£1,115)	(£1,620)	(£1,125)	(£630)	(£135)	£360	£855	£1,350	£1,845
Add sales receipt					1,000	1,000	1,000	1,000	1,000	1,000	1,000	1,000
Balance	400	(105)	(610)	(1,115)	(620)	(125)	370	865	1,360	1,855	2,350	2,845
Less Payments:												
Labour	450	450	450	450	450	450	450	450	450	450	450	450
Materials	15	15	15	15	15	15	15	15	15	15	15	15
Expenses	40	40	40	40	40	40	40	40	40	40	40	40
Total	£505	£505	£505	£505	£505	£505	£505	£505	£505	£505	£505	£505
Balance c/f	(105)	(610)	(1,115)	(1,620)	(1,125)	(630)	(135)	360	855	1,350	1,845	2,340

The cash budget clearly shows a cash-flow deficit for the first seven weeks, rising to a maximum of £1,620 in week 4. This might necessitate a change in the plan or it might be possible to obtain an overdraft facility of £2,000 for ten weeks from the bank. This will allow some flexibility if the plan has any errors in it.

Forecast profit and loss account

	£	£
Sales		12,000
Less Cost of sales:		
Opening inventory	6	
Add material purchased	180	
	186	
Less closing inventory	6	180
		11,820
Gross profit		
Less expenses:		
Wages	5,400	
Expenses	480	
		5,880
Net profit		£5,940

Balance sheet at the end of three months

	£		£
Inventory	6	Capital	406
Debtors	4,000	Profit	5,940
Bank	2,340		
	£6,346		£6,346

Chapter 16

The Cash Budget

As we saw in chapter 15, the cash budget is used to plan and control the cash balances on a day-to-day basis. Money, like the other resources employed in organizations, is costly and should not be allowed to sit around doing nothing. It should be continuously working, and to have too much lying around is as bad as having too little. The working capital is derived by taking the current liabilities away from the current assets of the organization, and is used to pay the running costs until more money is earned. The overall measure of the organization's liquidity and of its ability to pay its way is the amount of money it has readily available, which is generally represented by the cash in hand and cash at the bank.

In drawing up the cash budget the only figure that is known with absolute certainty is the opening balance, which is the amount of money that is in hand or overdrawn at the start of the budget period. The rest of the items are largely estimates, or informed guesses, based on past experience and taking into account present and expected conditions. The receipts from the sale of goods, or the number of hours' service provided, or rent for accommodation, will rarely be what is due or has been earned, but will rather be what has been earned minus late receipts of cash. For example, in a particular month a local authority may have charged rates of £70,000 but the payments received might be only £50,000. This sort of difference between what should be received and what is actually received should be catered for in the cash budget.

The same technique should be applied item by item, and those responsible for drawing up the budget should always remember that things will rarely happen exactly as they are planned. The government, with some of the best brains in the world at its disposal, was unable to get its forecast right when it launched the BP flotation, so ordinary mortals should not be too despondent when their plans go awry. Constant monitoring keeps any problems to a minimum.

Payments by organizations to their suppliers are just as likely to be delayed as receipts from customers, and it should be remembered that, within reasonable limits, organizations control when they make payments, whereas they do not have nearly so much control over when monies are received. Purchases may be paid for anything up to three months after the goods have been received, and some organizations wait even longer than that. The danger is that suppliers will become so tired of waiting for their money that any further goods are supplied on a cash-only basis or, what is perhaps worse, rumours will circulate that the organization is having cash-flow problems and people will refuse to deal with it at all. An extreme example of delayed payment would be purchases for one month, say, £20,000, payments for purchases £0, but this will generally occur only in the very early months of an organization, or when it is undergoing some sort of restructuring or other problem. More usually the figures would be something like purchases £20,000, payments £12,000.

The illustration of a cash budget in example 25 is not meant to be comprehensive but it does include many of the more usually encountered items. Once you have studied it, use a similar structure to solve exercise 21.

The budget shows a cash deficit of £12,000 at the end of December, but it should not cause too great a problem: if the cash budget has been closely monitored the organization will be aware of it in plenty of time to arrange an overdraft facility with the bank or other financing. If this proves impossible the organization may be able to delay some of the capital expenditure, or if none of these solutions is feasible it could be sold as a going concern before things got out of hand. Each month the actual position is compared with the plan, and to be useful the information must be available within at least a week of the month end and if possible sooner than that. Many undertakings monitor their cash on a daily basis and employ a computerized information system to enable them to do so.

Let us now apply the techniques of the cash budget to the role of the Personnel Manager. The Personnel Department is generally treated as a cost centre which provides little financial benefit to the organization. We have seen that this view can be challenged by an efficient Personnel Manager not only on the grounds of monies generated by selling training and recruitment facilities to outside organizations but also by demonstrating the savings that accrue when properly recruited and trained staff are working effectively. Indeed it might be argued that the Personnel Department is a profit centre rather than a cost centre.

The cash budget for a personnel department will employ exactly the

Example 25

Cash budget for three months to 31 December

	October Plan	October Actual	November Plan	November Actual	December Plan	December Actual
	£		£		£	
Opening balance in hand (overdrawn)	(4,000)		59,000		27,000	
Receipts from sales						
this month	80,000		90,000		88,000	
previous month	104,000		120,000		130,000	
Total	£180,000		£269,000		£245,000	
Less Payments for goods:						
this month	40,000		45,000		60,000	
previous month	50,000		60,000		70,000	
Wages and salaries	20,000		20,000		20,000	
Heating and lighting	–		–		4,000	
Transport	5,000		10,000		15,000	
Rates	–		–		10,000	
Capital items:						
Purchase of fixed assets	–		100,000		50,000	
Postage and stationery	2,000		1,000		2,000	
Telephones	3,000		4,000		5,000	
Loan interest	–		–		20,000	
Miscellaneous	1,000		2,000		1,000	
Total	£121,000		£242,000		£257,000	
Balance c/f in hand (overdrawn)	£ 59,000		£ 27,000		(£ 12,000)	

same principles as those already described but the headings might be slightly different. Such a cash budget might look like example 26.

Example 26

| | JANUARY | | FEBRUARY | | MARCH | |
	PLAN	ACTUAL	PLAN	ACTUAL	PLAN	ACTUAL
Opening balance						
RECEIPTS						
Training						
Recruitment						
PAYMENTS						
Employees						
Training						
Recruitment						
Travelling						
Materials						
Business rate						
Electricity						
Postage						
Telephone						
Services						
Capital						
Miscellaneous						
TOTAL						
Balance c/f						

By comparing the planned with the actual activity on a monthly basis, the Personnel Manager can ensure that effective corrective action is taken. Estimates of payments are generally speaking easier to make accurately than estimates of income, although with practice both will improve.

Exercise 21

Peter Brown intends to make and sell wooden models of famous sports personalities. Each model takes eight hours to make. Brown charges £8 per hour for his labour and uses mahogany costing £30; he adds 50% to the cost price to arrive at his selling price and feels that there is a market for his product. Research has made him believe that, once he is established and his product becomes known, he will be able to sell 10 models a week, and he would like to maintain a buffer stock of three of the most popular models. He gives four weeks' credit and anticipates the demand to be: week 1–3 no sales; weeks 4 and 5, six sales; weeks 6 onward, 10 sales. His other costs will be: rent of a shed, £10 per week; postage and stationery, £231 per week; rates, electricity and telephone, £1,200 per quarter, paid in March, June, September and December. The wood is purchased and paid for monthly in advance, with enough for forty models, and stored on racks in the shed. Brown has brought in £10,000 as capital, and he has bought equipment for £8,000, leaving a cash balance of £2,000. The business is to start on 1 January. Draw up the cash budget for the six months January to June, assuming that Brown withdraws £200 per week for living expenses and pays for additional equipment costing £5,000 in June. Would you recommend Brown to start the business?

Exercise 22

Use the skeleton budget given above to prepare a cash budget for your department. If you have difficulty arriving at some of the figures I am sure people in your organization will be pleased to help you.

Exercise 23

Draw up a cash budget from the following information for the six months from 1 July to 31 December.

- opening cash balance at 1 July £3,000
- sales at £40 per unit:

	April	May	June	July	Aug	Sept	Oct	Nov	Dec
units	220	240	280	320	360	380	260	160	140

- payment for goods two months after they have been sold
- £10 per unit direct labour payable in the same month as production
- raw materials £12 per unit, paid for three months after the goods are used in production
- production in units:

April	May	June	July	Aug	Sept	Oct	Nov	Dec	Jan
300	340	360	400	260	220	200	180	140	120

- other variable expenses £6 per unit, two-thirds paid for in the same month as production and one-third in the month following production

- fixed expenses £300 per month, paid one month in arrears
- capital expenditure for September £20,000

Exercise 24

The balance sheet of Dave's Delicatessen at 31st October is:

	£		£	£
Capital	13,750	Premises	10,000	
Creditors	3,000	Depreciation	2,000	
Overdraft	1,050			8,000
		Fittings	8,000	
		Depreciation	4,000	4,000
		Stock		5,000
		Debtors		800
	17,800			17,800

- sales are budgeted to be:

November	December	January	February	March	April
£6,000	£10,000	£7,000	£23,000	£4,000	£8,000

- Some sales are on credit and the proportions are on average 10 per cent credit, 90 per cent cash. Credit customers pay in the month following the sales.
- The gross profit margin is 25 per cent of selling price.
- Stocks are maintained at a constant level throughout the year.
- Fifty per cent of purchases are paid for in the same month as they are purchased and 50 per cent in the subsequent month.
- Wages and other running expenses are £2,000 per month paid in the month in which they are incurred.
- Premises and fittings are depreciated at 10 per cent per annum on cost.

Prepare a cash budget showing Dave's bank balance or overdraft for each month in the half year ending 30 April.

Solution 21

If the forecasts are correct and Brown can obtain an overdraft facility of £4,000 for six months the business seems likely to be successful. It should be borne in mind, however, that in order to produce 10 models he will have to work 80 hours a week and may find that impossible to achieve over a long period of time.

	January	February	March	April	May	June
Opening balance in hand (overdrawn)	£2,000	(£964)	(£3,082)	(£2,170)	£506	£3,182
Add receipts from sales		846	5,076	5,640	5,640	5,640
Total	£2,000	(£118)	£1,994	£3,470	£6,146	£8,822
Less Payments:						
Brown	800	800	800	800	800	800
Wood	1,200	1,200	1,200	1,200	1,200	1,200
Rent	40	40	40	40	40	40
Postage	924	924	924	924	924	924
Rates, etc			1,200			1,200
Equipment						5,000
Total	£2,964	£2,964	£4,164	£2,964	£2,964	£9,164
Balance c/f in hand (overdrawn)	(964)	(3,082)	(2,170)	506	3,182	(342)

Solution 23

	July	August	September	October	November	December
	£	£	£	£	£	£
Opening Balance	3,000	2,380	4,760	(10,660)	(4,600)	4,260
Sales receipts	9,600	11,200	12,800	14,400	15,200	10,400
	12,600	13,580	17,560	3,740	10,600	14,660
Payments:						
Labour	4,000	2,600	2,200	2,000	1,800	1,400
Materials	3,600	4,080	4,320	4,800	3,120	2,640
Variable expenses	720	800	520	440	400	360
Fixed expenses	1,600	1,040	880	800	720	560
Capital expenditure	–	–	20,000	–	–	–
	10,220	8,820	28,220	8,340	6,340	5,260
Balance carried forward	2,380	4,760	(10,660)	(4,600)	4,260	9,400

164

Solution 24

	November	December	January	February	March	April
	£	£	£	£	£	£
Opening Balance	(1,050)	(2,100)	(500)	(1,575)	6,575	350
Cash Receipts	5,400	9,000	6,300	20,700	3,600	7,200
Received from Debtors	800	600	1,000	700	2,300	400
	5,150	7,500	6,800	19,825	12,475	7,950
Cash	2,250	3,750	2,625	8,625	1,500	3,000
Previous Credit Purchases	3,000	2,250	3,750	2,625	8,625	1,500
Wages	2,000	2,000	2,000	2,000	2,000	2,000
	7,250	8,000	8,375	13,250	12,125	6,500
Balance carried forward	(2,100)	(500)	(1,575)	6,575	350	1,450

Chapter 17

The Master Budget

The master budget consists of the forecast trading and profit and loss account, balance sheet and cash statement. It draws on all the other budgets and can be completed only after they have been prepared. The budgeting process is a long drawn-out affair which takes up to nine months, and there are usually several attempts before the plan is finally agreed. There is a danger that people will become cynical about the process because they may have observed over the years, for example, that, whatever is set as the first budget, it is returned with a request that it should be pruned by 15 per cent. This makes them inflate the original plan by 15 per cent in the expectation that when the negotiations are completed they will receive the budget allocation they feel is necessary to allow them to function effectively.

Most budgets are set by looking at what has happened in the past and then adding whatever is necessary to keep up with inflation and extra needs, and this has the adverse effect of making people spend up to budget in the last month of two of a year, as they fear that any unspent money will be lost and as a consequence the budget for the next year will be reduced. Zero-based budgeting has been introduced as a means of avoiding this. This approach looks at the future needs of each budget centre and ignores anything that has happened in the past. The budget centre—which may be a branch, a department, a section or a product—is asked to submit its plan, and this is compared with requests from all the other budget centres before a decision is made. It is believed that this avoids the rush to spend up to budget before the year end, and so saves money.

This process of negotiation means that the master budget has to be prepared several times before it is complete, because the original plans may lead to a shortage of cash or a loss instead of a profit, and this information will be fed back into the system as illustrated on page 145, allowing the necessary revision to be made. The master budget allows the results of the planned activities to be expressed in the international language of finance, and provides a concise overall picture of the situation that can be readily assimilated and discussed by those concerned.

We have already seen that the budget for the Personnel Department is an integral part of this process. The Personnel Manager will have consulted with his or her staff to ascertain the likely level of activity over the forthcoming year for all aspects of the department's functions. Ideally these plans will be fully discussed within the department before they are finally submitted to the budget committee. If the department is to function effectively it is essential for all members to be fully committed to its objectives as stated in the budget and the best way to obtain this commitment is through involvement.

Different departmental managers have different approaches to the process and a great deal depends on the character of the individual involved. There is a danger in constantly asking for more or less than you require in order to run your department effectively in that you may well lose the respect of your colleagues. The manager who in the long term gains most from their negotiations is the one who makes careful estimates of future activities based on the information available at the time. There will of course be mistakes, but as long as they are seen and corrected early enough no major damage will be done.

Let us now consider the master budget of a manufacturing concern. The process followed is that illustrated in the model system in chapter 15. We will first show the budget and then explain how each of the individual items has been derived. This will be followed by the budget of a public authority.

Example 27

Forecast manufacturing account of Makes Co. for the year ending 30 June

	£	£
Opening inventory of raw materials		40,000
Add raw materials purchased		810,000
		850,000
Less closing inventory of raw materials		60,000
		790,000
Raw materials consumed		1,410,000
Direct manufacturing wages		10,000
Direct expenses		
Prime/direct cost of goods made		2,210,000
Add Indirect factory expenses/overheads:		
Salaries and wages	70,000	
Materials	30,000	
Heating and lighting	40,000	
Rent and rates	60,000	
Depreciation	90,000	
		290,000
Total manufacturing cost		2,500,000
Add opening work in progress		10,000
		2,510,000
Less closing work in progress		20,000
Cost of finished goods made		£2,490,000

Forecast trading and profit and loss account of Makes Co. for the year ending 30 June

	£	£
Sales		7,600,000
Less Cost of goods sold:		
Opening inventory of finished goods	40,000	
Add cost of goods manufactured	2,490,000	
	2,530,000	
Less closing inventory of finished goods	30,000	
		2,500,000
Gross profit		5,100,000
Less Expenses:		
Wages and salaries	3,750,000	
Selling and distribution	250,000	
Heating and lighting	40,000	
Depreciation	120,000	
Financing charges	65,000	
Miscellaneous	15,000	
		4,240,000
Net profit before tax		860,000

Budget Relationships

Opening inventory of raw materials ⎫	
Raw materials purchased ⎬	Materials budget
Closing inventory of raw materials ⎭	
Direct manufacturing wages	Labour budget
Direct expenses	Expenses budget
Salaries and wages	Labour budget
Materials ⎫	
Heating and lighting ⎬	Expenses budget
Rent and rates ⎭	
Depreciation	Capital assets budget
Work in progress ⎫	
Opening ⎬	Materials budget
Closing ⎭	
Sales	Activity budget
Opening inventory of finished goods ⎫	Finished goods budget
Closing inventory of finished goods ⎭	
Salaries and wages	Administration budget
Selling and distribution ⎫	Expenses budget
Heating and lighting ⎭	
Financing changes	Financial budget
Miscellaneous	Expenses budget
Land and buildings ⎫	
Plant and machinery ⎬	Capital asset budget
Motor vehicles ⎪	
Depreciation ⎭	
Inventory of raw materials ⎫	Materials budget
Inventory of work in progress ⎭	
Inventory of finished goods	Finished goods budget
Debtors	Activity budget
Bank	Cash budget
Capital	Master budget
Resources	Master budget
Loans	Financial budget
Creditors	Materials budget
Accruals	Expenses budget

Forecast balance sheet of Makes Co. as at 30 June

	£	£		£	£
Land and buildings	5,400,000		Capital		2,810,000
Less depreciation	2,300,000		Reserves		2,320,000
		3,100,000	Loans		500,000
Plant and machinery	1,960,000				
Less depreciation	660,000				
		1,300,000			
Motor vehicles	320,000				
Less depreciation	60,000				
		260,000			
Current assets:			Current liabilities:		
Inventory of raw materials	60,000		Creditors	70,000	
Inventory of work in progress	20,000		Accruals	20,000	
Inventory of finished goods	30,000				90,000
	110,000				
Debtors	940,000				
Bank	10,000				
		1,060,000			
		5,720,000			5,720,000

Example 28

Budget of a public authority

General Fund Summary

Actual 1992/93 £	Original Estimate 1993/94 £	Revised Estimate 1993/94 £		Estimate 1994/95 £
358,755	603,440	476,300	Economic Development	502,930
5,815,952	6,265,080	6,317,390	Environment	6,533,470
3,146,942	3,813,000	3,438,620	Housing (General Fund)	3,724,000
9,259,434	9,454,600	9,263,290	Leisure	9,599,220
2,243,565	2,235,400	2,396,000	Arts, Museums & Festival	2,131,410
2,608,601	2,544,070	2,433,490	Planning	2,467,040
			Policy & Resources	
6,804	3,000	16,380	Caen Panel	17,210
(2,875,855)	(3,710,600)	(3,997,400)	Commercial Docks Board	(3,163,400)
(146,064)	10,660	(246,000)	Contract Services Board – trading accounts	(150,000)
299,265	–	35,000	– redundancy costs	–
(15,358)	(28,030)	(20,490)	Licensing	(1,700)
–	187,320	140,730	Professional Services Board	(18,730)
4,054,676	3,956,340	5,001,090	Resources Management	4,717,650
11,287	155,000	330,610	Special Events 1994	572,410
1,812,985	2,007,630	2,158,350	Traffic and Transportation	2,131,470
(1,744,895)	(1,888,730)	(2,317,600)	Reduced debt repayments	(2,417,650)
24,836,094	25,608,180	25,425,760	**COMMITTEE EXPENDITURE**	26,645,330
			OTHER EXPENDITURE/(INCOME)	
490	490	490	Housing Revenue Account (Other)	490
26,033	30,000	20,000	Apprentice training	15,000
362,572	(3,660)	(118,300)	Insurance reserve – net (surplus)/deficit	(100,320)
68,539	(400,000)	(310,000)	Vehicle reserve – net purchases	(209,000)
34,197	–	–	Caen Foundation – earmarked reserve	–
300,000	50,000	50,000	Provision for doubtful debts	50,000
(135,053)	–	–	De minimis capital receipts	–
74,673	74,500	74,500	Precepts	76,000
–	581,240	100,000	Contingency	500,000
–	–	–	Provision for potential pay awards	320,000
–	–	(275,520)	Civic Properties – reduction in rateable values	–
100,339	–	–	Rate income account deficit	–
(464,756)	1,313,820	837,230	Interest on use of cash balances	881,290
25,203,128	27,254,570	25,804,160	**TOTAL (NET) EXPENDITURE**	28,178,790
			FINANCED BY:	
8,167,248	1,543,470	93,060	Contribution from/(to) balances and reserves	2,479,950
	15,191,580	15,191,580	Revenue Support Grant	15,420,850
	6,490,390	6,490,390	Business Rate income	6,109,020
17,035,880	4,029,130	4,029,130	Collection Fund	4,168,970
25,203,128	27,254,570	25,804,160		28,178,790
			BALANCES & RESERVES	
13,851,946	4,216,725	5,684,698	Balance brought forward at 1 April	5,591,638
(8,167,248)	(1,543,470)	(93,060)	Deduct deficit for the year	(2,479,950)
5,684,698	2,673,255	5,591,638	Balance carried forward at 31 March	3,111,688

ANALYSIS OF BALANCES & RESERVES

	General Balances £	Docks £	Vehicle £	Redundancy £	Insurance £	Swimming Pool (Rev.) £	Other £	TOTAL £
1 April '93	3,177,704	935,788	319,200	310,797	438,786	–	502,423	5,684,698
Used 1993/94	581,207	(135,788)	(319,200)	189,203	61,214	–	(469,696)	(93,060)
31 March '94	3,758,911	800,000	0	500,000	500,000	–	32,727	5,591,638
Used 1994/95	(2,763,250)	0	–	–	–	300,000	(16,700)	(2,479,950)
31 March '95	995,661	800,000	0	500,000	500,000	300,000	16,027	3,111,688

Calculation of the Council Tax 1994/95

Portsmouth City Council	1994/95 £	1993/94 £
Gross Expenditure	161,320,011	146,277,193
LESS Gross Income	135,621,171	120,566,093
Net Expenditure 1994/95	**25,698,840**	25,711,100
LESS Revenue Support Grant/NDR Pool contribution	21,529,870	21,681,970
Standard Spending Assessment Reduction Grant	668,630	–
	3,500,340	4,029,130
ADD Deficit on Collection Fund at 31 March 1994	670,500	512,703
Net Budget Requirement – Portsmouth City Council Purposes	**4,170,840**	4,541,833
Council Tax Base	54,145.7	53,065
Council Tax – Portsmouth City Council Purposes at Band D $\frac{4,170,840}{54,145.7}$ =	**77.03**	£85.59

Hampshire County Council Precept	22,786,676	19,600,088
Council Tax – Hampshire County Council Purposes at Band D	**£420.84**	£369.36

The Council Tax to be levied for all bands in 1994/95 will be as follows:

Estimated Valuation at 1 April 1991	Band	Hampshire County Council £	Portsmouth City Council £	TOTAL £	1993/94 £
Up to £40,000	A	280.56	51.35	331.91	303.30
£40,001 – £52,000	B	327.32	59.91	387.23	353.85
£52,001 – £68,000	C	374.08	68.47	442.55	404.40
£68,001 – £88,000	D	420.84	77.03	497.87	454.95
£88,001 – £120,000	E	514.36	94.15	608.51	556.05
£120,001 – £160,000	F	607.88	111.27	719.15	657.15
£160,001 – £320,000	G	701.40	128.38	829.78	758.25
£320,000 and over	H	841.68	154.06	995.74	909.90

174 Finance and Accounting for Managers

From these examples it can be seen that the budgetary control system is totally integrated and can be of use to the organization only as long as it remains so. If any one budget endeavours to stand on its own the system becomes useless. The way in which the budget is drawn up from basic information is shown in chapter 15, which should be studied in conjunction with this chapter.

Chapter 18

Capital Budgeting Systems

All systems of budgetary control are important and require the utmost care in their preparation and monitoring, but whilst revenue budgets commit an organization for only a short period of time, normally one year, capital schemes can commit them to expenditure for ten or more years. The capital budget of an organization in its original draft may be drawn up on similar lines to example 29 (see page 176) for the next ten years.

The budget committee would focus most strongly on years 1 and 2, but as organizations face more demands on their resources than can be met, some method of deciding which among competing schemes should go forward for further consideration has to be devised. It is important to emphasize that the methods of helping to eliminate some schemes do not in themselves make the decision; all they do is give the decision-maker additional information on which to act.

There are three generally accepted methods of capital rationing, that is, of helping decide which schemes should be allowed to go forward for further consideration: pay-back, rate of return and discounted cash flow.

Pay-back

This enables the time taken to recover the initial investment—either through additional money coming into the organization or by reducing the cash outflow—to be calculated. The result can then be compared with the desired pay-back period, which might be three years. Schemes that meet the criterion—i.e. that have a pay-back of three years or less—go forward for consideration, whilst the others are excluded. Example 30 shows such a system of pay-back.

Example 29

Project	Total £(000)	Year 1 £(000)	Year 2 £(000)	Year 3 £(000)	Year 4 £(000)	Year 5 £(000)	Year 6 £(000)	Year 7 £(000)	Year 8 £(000)	Year 9 £(000)	Year 10 £(000)
A	22,300	4,000	8,000	10,000	300						
B	22,290			400	900	7,500	12,800	690			
C	650	600	50								
D	16,000	12,500	2,500	1,000							
E	33,200	7,000	200	9,000	8,000	6,000	2,400	600			
F	24,000										
G	43,800			7,000	15,000	20,000	1,200	500			
H	33,700		7,600	19,400	6,200	500					
I	8,000				8,000				4,000	8,000	12,000
J	40	40							100		
K	10	10									
L	60	60									
M	15		15								
TOTAL	204,065	24,210	18,365	46,800	38,400	34,000	16,400	1,790	4,100	8,000	12,000

Example 30

The Personnel Department requires a piece of machinery that costs £30,000 and is more efficient than the existing machine, resulting in an annual saving in operating costs, excluding depreciation, over five years of £6,000 in year 1, £8,000 in year 2 and £10,000 in years 3–5. The pay-back in this case, provided the savings are generated equally throughout the year, would be:

Cost		£30,000
Pay-back		*Cumulative*
Year 1	£ 6,000	£ 6,000
Year 2	8,000	14,000
Year 3	10,000	24,000
Year 4 (7·2 months)	6,000	30,000

In this case pay-back takes three years and 7·2 months, so that if the three years' pay-back was the sole criterion the scheme would not go forward for further consideration.

Budget holders are concerned with the speed at which their outlay is recovered, so this method of capital rationing is frequently met in practice. It is easy to understand and apply, but it has the disadvantage of ignoring what happens once pay-back has been achieved and does not review the scheme as a whole. On the other hand, it has the advantage of recognizing, even if only indirectly, that money recovered earlier is more valuable than money received later, because money that you have can be invested and earn interest.

Rate of return

Applying the rate of return to the example 30, we have:

$$\text{Outlay} \qquad £30,000$$

Average annual cash flow:

$$\frac{£6,000 + £8,000 + £10,000 + £10,000 + £10,000}{5 \text{ years}} = \frac{£44,000}{5}$$

$$= £8,800 \text{ p.a.}$$

The average annual cash flow of £8,800 is expressed as a percentage of the outlay of £30,000:

$$= \frac{£8,800 \times 100}{£30,000} = 29 \cdot 3\%$$

If the organization was looking for a return of 30 per cent this scheme would be excluded, but if 25 per cent was the required rate it would go forward for further consideration. This method is not as commonly employed as the pay-back, although it is relatively easy to understand and apply and it does review the whole scheme. Its disadvantage is that it ignores the time value of money, that is, £1 received today is treated as having the same value as £1 received in ten years' time, which is nonsense in view of the opportunities of investing the money available now.

Discounted cash flow (net present value)

Applying discounted cash flow techniques to arrive at the net present value of the scheme, and assuming that the organization requires a 16 per cent return on investment, we have:

Outlay			£30,000
Savings:			
Year 1	£ 6,000 × 0·8621	= 5172·6	
Year 2	£ 8,000 × 0·7432	= 5945·6	
Year 3	£10,000 × 0·6407	= 6407	
Year 4	£10,000 × 0·5523	= 5523	
Year 5	£10,000 × 0·4761	= 4761	
Present value of the future cash flows			£27,809·2
Net present value of scheme			− £ 2,190·8

In this calculation the discount figure of 0·8621 in year 1, and those for the other years, are obtained from discount tables like those in the Appendix. The relevant table is the 16 per cent table, and the column used is 'Present value of £1'. This process can be considerably speeded up when the same sum of money is involved in each year, because it is then possible to use the 'Present value of £1 received at the end of period' column just once, as has been done in solution 26.

The present value of the future cash flows is less than the outlay of £30,000, which means that the scheme is not making the required 16 per cent on the investment and should not go forward for further consideration. This approach to capital rationing is frequently employed because it reviews the whole scheme and recognizes the time value of money. Tables are prepared showing the appropriate rate to multiply by at various time intervals and costs of money.

There is a growing tendency for organizations to use a combination of pay-back and net present value in capital rationing when preparing their capital budgets, but it should be borne in mind that, although capital budgeting is essential, a great deal of capital expenditure takes place on the basis of pure necessity rather than because it has been planned for. Machinery breaks down or has to be replaced by new technology, so it should always be remembered that the budget is a plan and not a straitjacket. Different people need different things to help them in their planning, decision making and control, and it is essential that the management information system gives the right information to the right people and at the right time. The Personnel Manager needs to keep in mind the criteria that have to be met before schemes requiring capital expenditure are agreed, otherwise all proposals for capital expenditure in the department may be rejected. The effective manager will ensure the department proposals for capital expenditure meet the required pay-back, rate of return or discounted cash flow requirements measures. It is no use to propose outlay on new equipment that will provide training more effectively if the pay-back is five years whilst the organization requires three years. Neither would a return of 8 per cent be considered if the organization expects 10 per cent. To keep submitting schemes that fail to meet the hurdle rates simply ruins the credibility of the department and is in no one's interest because the organization as a whole suffers from the inefficiencies of a major constituent.

Work through the following exercises and compare your answers with those suggested.

Exercise 25

Green is concerned about production costs and after extensive enquiries has identified a new machine that will carry out the required process much more effectively than his present one. The machine costs £80,000 and will last for eight years, during which time running costs and maintenance will be reduced by £10,000 a year and there will be a saving on materials of £4,000 a year. Would you recommend Green to buy the machine if the only consideration was a financial one and the cost of money was 15 per cent?

Exercise 26

A local authority has decided that the heating costs of the Personnel Department are excessive and has received tenders for insulating the building. The costs of insulation are £130,000, inclusive of double glazing and it is expected that the benefits will last for fifteen years, after which the department will move to new premises. The estimated savings from the insulation are £16,000 a year and the cost of capital is 8 per cent. Should the insulation be undertaken on the basis of the financial information provided?

Solution 25

	Pay-back	
Cost of new machine		£80,000
Annual savings	£14,000	
Pay-back	5·7 years	

If Green is looking for a three-year pay-back the scheme would be rejected. The decision would be reversed, however, if he required a six-year pay-back.

	Rate of return	
Cost of new machine		£80,000
Average annual savings	£14,000	

As the same sum of money is saved each year the average annual saving is the same as the annual saving.

$$\text{Rate of return} = \frac{£14,000 \times 100}{£80,000} = 17\cdot5\%$$

If Green requires a 15 per cent rate of return this scheme could go forward.

	Discounted cash flow	£
Cost of new machine		80,000
Savings:		
1	£14,000 × 0·8696 = £12,174·4	
2	14,000 × 0·7561 = 10,585·4	
3	14,000 × 0·6575 = 9,205·0	
4	14,000 × 0·5718 = 8,005·2	
5	14,000 × 0·4972 = 6,960·8	
6	14,000 × 0·4323 = 6,052·2	
7	14,000 × 0·3759 = 5,262·6	
8	14,000 × 0·3269 = 4,576·6	
Present value of future cash flows		62,822·2
Net present value of scheme		− 17,177·8

The scheme would be rejected on this criterion, as it would not make the 15 per cent required, but there may be criteria other than the financial one that could make Green decide to go ahead anyway, for example his competitive position.

In using the discounted cash flow (DCF) approach it is possible to take a short cut when the same sum of money is involved each year. So far we have used the 'Present value of £1' column but we could use the 'Present value of £1 received at end of period' column, when we have:

		£
Cost of new machine		80,000
Savings	14,000 × 4·4873	
Present value of future cash flows		62,822·2
Net present value of the scheme		− 17,177·8

It should be emphasized that this approach can be employed only when the same sum of money is involved each year.

Solution 26

	Pay-back	
Cost of insulation		£130,000
Savings	£ 16,000 p.a.	
Pay-back	£130,000	
	£ 16,000 =	8·1 years

If the authority requires a pay-back of five years this scheme would be rejected but if the criterion was ten years it could go forward.

	Rate of return	£
Cost of insulation		130,000
Average annual savings		16,000

Rate of return	$\dfrac{£16,000 \times 100}{£130,000} =$	12·3%

If a return of 8 per cent is required this scheme could proceed but 14 per cent would cause it to be rejected.

	Discounted cash flow	£
Cost of insulation		130,000
Savings	£16,000 × 8·5595	
Present value of future cash flows		136,952
Net present value of the scheme		+ 6,952

The scheme would be accepted, as it would make more than the 8 per cent required.

Chapter 19

Operating Parameters

In looking at the financial information systems that are available to help organizations in decision making, planning and control, we have so far ignored the fact that there is a legal framework within which they must operate, irrespective of whether they are in the public or the private sector. There are constraints relating to terms and conditions of employment, unfair dismissal and equal opportunities, all of which generally come under the auspices of the Personnel Manager, as do disciplinary and grievance procedures. The purpose of this chapter is to introduce a little of the legal framework, but it should be borne in mind that this is an important area; more detailed discussion can be found in David Lewis's *Essentials of Employment Law* (2nd edition, 1994) and the books in the IPD's Law and Employment series. The private and public sectors will be considered in turn.

The private sector

This contains three types of business organization.

Sole trader

This type of organization, as the name implies, consists of a single individual who takes full responsibility for all the work that is undertaken. If things go well, and the business is successful, all the profits can be taken and used as the proprietor chooses. On the other hand, if things go badly, and losses are incurred, all his personal effects including the family home can be called upon to repay creditors.

The sole trader can commence business at any time, with few formalities. It is however, usual to register for value added tax (VAT), and to obtain any necessary planning permission. If the owner wishes to use a company name that differs from his or her own name then the

Business Names Act, 1985, has to be complied with. The business ceases with the death or retirement of the owner.

Partnerships

A partnership consists of two or more people who agree to carry on a business, sharing profits and losses in proportions that are the subject of discussion between them. The partnership agreement may be purely verbal, but it is usually in writing. It sets out the way in which profits and losses are to be shared as well as any salaries that are to be received by the partners. The partnership, like the sole trader, can start business at any time with few formalities other than the necessity of obtaining any necessary planning permission, registering for VAT and complying with the Business Names Act, 1985.

The death of a partner can lead to the dissolution of the partnership, but more usually the agreement will provide for the business to continue under the remaining partner(s). It will be necessary for the continuing partner(s) to buy out the share of the deceased, with consequent problems in raising finance. The basic rules which apply to a partnership are found in the Partnership Act, 1890, which, together with the general law of the land, governs its activities.

Companies

There are two types of company, the limited (Ltd), which is not allowed to offer its shares to the general public and the public limited company (PLC) whose shares are offered to the public at large through the medium of the Stock Exchange. Both types of organization consist of two or more people incorporated as a registered company, who become its shareholders and appoint directors to manage the company and act as its agents. The shareholders must also appoint a company secretary. The company cannot commence business until the formalities have been completed. They include a certificate of incorporation from the Registrar of Companies, compliance with the Companies Act, 1985, the Business Names Act, 1985, and usually registration for VAT.

The company has a separate legal entity from the owners, and its existence is unaffected by the death or retirement of any of them. On the other hand, it has a far more complex legal environment in which to operate than either the sole trader or the partnership. It has an obligation to file accounts annually, together with the directors' and auditors' reports. These items are retained by the Registrar of Companies, and are available for inspection on request from Companies House. Annual general meetings must be held, so that shareholders are kept informed of corporate activities and, in addition, the articles and memorandum of association set out the limits of the company's activities in pursuance of its trade.

The public sector

This contains three types of organization: the commercial public organization, the social services organization and the local government organization.

Commercial public corporations

These receive their authority and constraints from the government, and are run on commercial lines under the control of a minister.

Social service organizations

These also receive their authority from the government, on whose behalf they run a social service, such as the Health and Safety Executive.

The commercial public corporations and social service organizations each have a separate legal entity, and their objects and powers are contained in the Act of Parliament which created them.

Local authorities

These derive their powers and limitations from the Acts of Parliament and charters that created them. They have a great many obligatory duties and enormous permissive powers, but they must take great care that they do nothing that is *ultra vires*, i.e. outside their powers, for if they do they have to pay for the consequences. They are independent within the powers authorized by the central government.

The public-sector organizations employ large numbers of people, so that the death or retirement of an individual has no effect on their existence. They have a statutory duty to account for the manner in which they discharge their responsibilities, and must appoint auditors to report on the activities of the period under review. Accounts have to be prepared for the central government, which are open to inspection by the general public. In recent years the government's concern to obtain value for money has put local authorities under close public scrutiny. As a result, they are considered to have become more efficient.

The conditions under which such organizations operate are complex, and all are restricted in what they are legally entitled to do. This makes it essential for them to take legal advice when they are established, to help ensure that the purpose for which they have been set up is a legitimate one. This will help to see that they enjoy the confidence of the general public that they serve.

Appendix

Discounted Cash Flow: Selected Tables

Only those sections of a full set of tables that relate to chapter 18 are shown here.

Year	Amount to which £1 will accumulate	Present value of £1	Present value of £1 received at end of period	Present value of £1 received continuously	Amount received at end of year which will recover initial investment of £1	Amount received continuously which will recover initial investment of £1	Year
8 per cent rate of return							
1	1·0800	0·9259	0·9259	0·9625	1·0800	1·0390	1
2	1·1664	0·8573	1·7833	1·8537	0·5608	0·5395	2
3	1·2597	0·7938	2·5771	2·6789	0·3880	0·3733	3
4	1·3605	0·7350	3·3121	3·4429	0·3019	0·2905	4
5	1·4693	0·6806	3·9927	4·1504	0·2505	0·2409	5
6	1·5869	0·6302	4·6229	4·8054	0·2163	0·2081	6
7	1·7138	0·5835	5·2064	5·4120	0·1921	0·1848	7
8	1·8509	0·5403	5·7466	5·9736	0·1740	0·1674	8
9	1·9990	0·5002	6·2469	6·4936	0·1601	0·1540	9
10	2·1589	0·4632	6·7101	6·9750	0·1490	0·1434	10
11	2·3316	0·4289	7·1390	7·4209	0·1401	0·1348	11
12	2·6182	0·3971	7·5361	7·8337	0·1327	0·1277	12
13	2·7196	0·3677	7·9038	8·2159	0·1265	0·1217	13
14	2·9372	0·3405	8·2442	8·5698	0·1213	0·1167	14

Year	Amount to which £1 will accumulate	Present value of £1	Present value of £1 received at end of period	Present value of £1 received continuously	Amount received at end of year which will re-cover initial investment of £1	Amount received continuously which will re-cover initial investment of £1	Year
15	3·1722	0·3152	8·5595	8·8975	0·1168	0·1124	15
16	3·4259	0·2919	8·8514	9·2009	0·1150	0·1087	16
17	3·7000	0·2703	9·1216	9·4818	0·1096	0·1055	17
18	3·9960	0·2502	9·3719	9·7420	0·1067	0·1026	18
19	4·3157	0·2317	9·6036	9·9828	0·1041	0·1002	19
20	4·6610	0·2145	9·8181	10·2058	0·1019	0·0980	20
21	5·0338	0·1987	10·0168	10·4123	0·0998	0·0960	21
22	5·4365	0·1839	10·2007	10·6035	0·0980	0·0943	22
23	5·8715	0·1703	10·3711	10·7806	0·0964	0·0928	23
24	6·3412	0·1577	10·5288	10·9445	0·0950	0·0914	24
25	6·8485	0·1460	10·6748	11·0963	0·0937	0·0901	25

15 per cent rate of return

Year	Amount to which £1 will accumulate	Present value of £1	Present value of £1 received at end of period	Present value of £1 received continuously	Amount received at end of year which will re-cover initial investment of £1	Amount received continuously which will re-cover initial investment of £1	Year
1	1·1500	0·8696	0·8696	0·9333	1·1500	1·0715	1
2	1·3225	0·7561	1·6257	1·7448	0·6151	0·5731	2
3	1·5209	0·6575	2·2832	2·4505	0·4380	0·4081	3
4	1·7490	0·5718	2·8550	3·0641	0·3503	0·3264	4
5	2·0114	0·4972	3·3522	3·5977	0·2983	0·2780	5
6	2·3131	0·4323	3·7845	4·0617	0·2642	0·2462	6
7	2·6600	0·3759	4·1604	4·4652	0·2404	0·2240	7
8	3·0590	0·3269	4·4873	4·8160	0·2229	0·2076	8
9	3·5179	0·2843	4·7716	5·1211	0·2096	0·1953	9

n							n
10	4·0456	0·2472	5·0188	5·3864	0·1993	0·1857	10
11	4·6524	0·2149	5·2337	5·6171	0·1911	0·1780	11
12	5·3503	0·1869	5·4206	5·8177	0·1845	0·1719	12
13	6·1528	0·1625	5·5831	5·9921	0·1791	0·1669	13
14	7·0757	0·1413	5·7245	6·1438	0·1747	0·1628	14
15	8·1371	0·1229	5·8474	6·2757	0·1710	0·1593	15
16	9·3576	0·1069	5·9542	6·3904	0·1679	0·1565	16
17	10·7613	0·0929	6·0472	6·4901	0·1654	0·1541	17
18	12·3755	0·0808	6·1280	6·5769	0·1632	0·1520	18
19	14·2318	0·0703	6·1982	6·6523	0·1613	0·1503	19
20	16·3665	0·0611	6·2593	6·7178	0·1598	0·1489	20
21	18·8215	0·0531	6·3125	6·7749	0·1584	0·1476	21
22	21·6447	0·0462	6·3587	6·8245	0·1573	0·1465	22
23	24·8915	0·0402	6·3988	6·8676	0·1563	0·1456	23
24	28·6252	0·0349	6·4338	6·9051	0·1554	0·1448	24
25	32·9190	0·0304	6·4641	6·9377	0·1547	0·1441	25

16 per cent rate of return

n							n
1	1·1600	0·8621	0·8621	0·9293	1·1600	1·0760	1
2	1·3456	0·7432	1·6052	1·7305	0·6230	0·5779	2
3	1·5609	0·6407	2·2459	2·4211	0·4453	0·4130	3
4	1·8106	0·5523	2·7982	3·0165	0·3574	0·3315	4
5	2·1003	0·4761	3·2743	3·5298	0·3054	0·2833	5
6	2·4364	0·4104	3·6847	3·9722	0·2714	0·2517	6
7	2·8262	0·3538	4·0386	4·3537	0·2476	0·2297	7
8	3·2784	0·3050	4·3436	4·6825	0·2302	0·2136	8
9	3·8030	0·2630	4·6065	4·9660	0·2171	0·2014	9
10	4·4114	0·2267	4·8332	5·2103	0·2069	0·1919	10

Glossary

Accounting period   Normally twelve months as far as the financial accounts are concerned, to coincide with the tax year. So far as the management accounts are concerned it can be any period ranging from one week to one year. It is generally thought necessary to provide management information at least once every four weeks.

Acid test   Test of the ability of an organization to pay its way in the short term, given by the ratio of quick assets to current liabilities.

Added value   The value an organization adds to bought-in goods and services. It goes to meet wages and then profits.

Articles of association   Internal rules that state the rights and duties of directors and shareholders of a company.

Assets   Items belonging to the organization that have either a long-term or a short-term value. Those having a long-term value are items like machinery and plant. They are called fixed assets.

Authorized capital   The total amount of money that the organization is authorized to raise by the issue of share capital. The authorized capital is subject to stamp duty, and so organizations do not state high authorized capital figures when they are first formed. The authorized share capital is not set for all time, and can be varied if necessary.

Book value   The value at which an asset is shown in the balance sheet.

Budget   A forecast or estimate of events over a stated future interval of time, e.g. one year, five years or six months.

Capital employed   The total of the assets owned. The net capital employed is more usually used in calculating ratios and is the total assets less the current liabilities.

Capital items   Items that last for several years. Examples are machinery used in manufacture, motor vehicles, land and buildings.

Credit terms   Terms allowing for payment for goods will be made at a later date.

Current assets   Assets that are normally used up in one financial period and change from day to day.

Current liabilities   Liabilities that must be settled within a short time; they fluctuate from day to day.

Current ratio   Measure of the organization's ability to pay its way in the period between about three and nine months in the future. Given by the ratio of current assets to current liabilities.

Debenture   A certificate issued by a company acknowledging a debt.

Depreciation   Method of allocating the cost of a fixed asset over its useful life.

Discounted cash flow (DCF)   Future cash flows discounted to give their present value.

Dividend   Distribution of profits to the shareholders. Usually expressed as a dividend of *x*p in the £ on the nominal value of shares.

Earnings   Money received or due for goods or services provided by the organization.

Equity   The part of a business that belongs to the owners. It is what remains after all outside interests have received their money.

Expenses   Money paid or due to be paid by the organization for revenue, goods or services it has received.

Fixed assets   Assets held for many years to earn profits. Examples are land and buildings, or plant and machinery.

Fixed overheads   Expenses that do not vary with the level of activity.

Gearing   Relationship between the share capital and loan capital of a business.

Goodwill   The excess over the book value of a business that is received when the business is sold.

Historical cost   The cost at which the assets were obtained.

Income statement   Used to calculate the profit or loss of an organization in an accounting period. Made up of: (1) The *manufacturing account*, showing the costs of goods made; (2) The *trading account*, showing the gross profit or loss; the difference between the cost price and selling price of the goods; (3) the *profit and loss account*, showing the net profit or loss.

Inventory   Stock.

Issued capital   The shares that have been issued by the organization in order to raise money.

Job cost   Cost of a single job or operation.

Liabilities   Money that the organization owes.

Long-term liabilities   Long-term debts.

Margin of safety   The excess of sales over the break-even point.

Marginal cost   The cost of one more unit.

Memorandum of association   Constitution of a company.

Net assets   Total assets less current liabilities.

Net capital employed   The resources that are employed in the business for more than one year; enables the return on the long-term investment to be found. The net capital employed is calculated by deducting the current liabilities from the total assets.

NPV   Net present value of a scheme.

Ordinary shares   Share capital that has a fixed rate of dividend, and receives its dividends before the rest of the share capital.

Prime costs   Direct materials, direct labour and direct expenses added together.

Profit   Surplus of earnings over expenses.

Public limited company (PLC)   Limited company that conforms to European Union regulations.

Quick assets   Assets that are quickly and easily realizable—normally debtors and cash.

Quick ratio   Acid test.

Reserves   Profits that are retained in the business—rarely cash.

Retained profits   Reserves.

Revenue items   Items that are completely used up or discharged in one year. Examples are salaries, wages, heating, raw materials.

Revenue reserves   Reserves distributable to shareholders.

Share capital   The amount received from the shareholders of the business.

Share premium   A capital reserve (one which cannot be distributed to the shareholders) created when the company sells its shares at a price in excess of the nominal value.

Standard cost   Predetermined or expected cost.

Stock turnover   Number of times the stock is turned over in a financial period, given by the ratio of goods sold to cost of stock.

Turnover   Total sales value.

Variable overheads   Indirect expenses that vary with the level of activity.

Variances   Differences between standard and actual performance.

Working capital   Capital needed to keep the business operating until more money is obtained from operations. It is current assets minus current liabilities.

Bibliography

BIERMAN, H., and SMIDT, S., *The Capital Budgeting Decision*, fifth edition, New York, Macmillan; London, Collier Macmillan, 1980

BULL., R. J., *Accounting in Business*, fourth edition, Butterworth, London, 1980

CLARKSON, C. P. E., and ELLIOTT, B. J., *Managing Money and Finance*, Gower, Aldershot, 1983

DAVIES, D. B., *The Art of Managing Finance*, second edition, McGraw-Hill, London, 1992

FAIR, H., *Personnel and Profit: The pay-off from people*, IPM, London, 1992

GOCH, D., *Finance and Accounts for Managers*, revised edition, Pan, London, 1980

HARTLEY, W. C. F., *Introduction to Business Accounting for Managers*, third edition, Pergamon, Oxford, 1980

HATHERLEY, D., *Accounting for Business Activity*, Pitman, London, 1993

HENLEY, D. *et al.*, *Public Sector Accounting and Financial Control*, fourth edition, Chapman and Hall, London, 1992

HORNGREN, C. T., *Cost Accounting—A Managerial Emphasis*, fifth edition, Prentice-Hall, London, 1982

Key British Enterprises (annual edition), Dunn and Bradstreet, London, 1990

LAUDERBACK, J. G., and HIRSCH, M. L., *Cost Accounting*, Kent, Boston, Mass., 1982

LEWIS, D., *Essentials of Employment Law*, second edition, IPM, London, 1994

SAMUELS, J. M., and WILKES, F. M., *Management of Company Finance*, third edition, Nelson, Walton on Thames, 1980

TAYLOR, A. H., and PALMER, R. E., *Financial Planning for Managers*, revised edition, Pan, London, 1980

WATTS, J., *Accounting in the Business Environment*, Pitman, London, 1993

Index